Principles
in Practice

The Principles in Practice imprint offers teachers concrete illustrations of effective classroom practices based in NCTE research briefs and policy statements. Each book discusses the research on a specific topic, links the research to an NCTE brief or policy statement, and then demonstrates how those principles come alive in practice: by showcasing actual classroom practices that demonstrate the policies in action; by talking about research in practical, teacher-friendly language; and by offering teachers possibilities for rethinking their own practices in light of the ideas presented in the books. Books within the imprint are grouped in strands, each strand focused on a significant topic of interest.

Adolescent Literacy Strand

Adolescent Literacy at Risk? The Impact of Standards (2009) Rebecca Bowers Sipe

Adolescents and Digital Literacies: Learning Alongside Our Students (2010) Sara Kajder

Adolescent Literacy and the Teaching of Reading: Lessons for Teachers of Literature (2010) Deborah Appleman

Rethinking the "Adolescent" in Adolescent Literacy (2017) Sophia Tatiana Sarigianides, Robert Petrone, and Mark A. Lewis

Restorative Justice in the English Language Arts Classroom (2019) Maisha T. Winn, Hannah Graham, and Rita Renjitham Alfred

Writing in Today's Classrooms Strand

Writing in the Dialogical Classroom: Students and Teachers Responding to the Texts of Their Lives (2011) Bob Fecho

Becoming Writers in the Elementary Classroom: Visions and Decisions (2011) Katie Van Sluys

Writing Instruction in the Culturally Relevant Classroom (2011) Maisha T. Winn and Latrise P. Johnson

Writing Can Change Everything: Middle Level Kids Writing Themselves into the World (2020) Shelbie Witte, editor

Literacy Assessment Strand

Our Better Judgment: Teacher Leadership for Writing Assessment (2012) Chris W. Gallagher and Eric D. Turley

Beyond Standardized Truth: Improving Teaching and Learning through Inquiry-Based Reading Assessment (2012) Scott Filkins

Reading Assessment: Artful Teachers, Successful Students (2013) Diane Stephens, editor

Going Public with Assessment: A Community Practice Approach (2018) Kathryn Mitchell Pierce and Rosario Ordoñez-Jasis

Literacies of the Disciplines Strand

Entering the Conversations: Practicing Literacy in the Disciplines (2014) Patricia Lambert Stock, Trace Schillinger, and Andrew Stock

Real-World Literacies: Disciplinary Teaching in the High School Classroom (2014) Heather Lattimer

Doing and Making Authentic Literacies (2014) Linda Denstaedt, Laura Jane Roop, and Stephen Best

Reading in Today's Classrooms Strand

Connected Reading: Teaching Adolescent Readers in a Digital World (2015) Kristen Hawley Turner and Troy Hicks

Digital Reading: What's Essential in Grades 3–8 (2015) William L. Bass II and Franki Sibberson

Teaching Reading with YA Literature: Complex Texts, Complex Lives (2016) Jennifer Buehler

Teaching English Language Learners Strand

Beyond "Teaching to the Test": Rethinking Accountability and Assessment for English Language Learners (2017) Betsy Gilliland and Shannon Pella

Community Literacies en Confianza: *Learning from Bilingual After-School Programs* (2017) Steven Alvarez

Understanding Language: Supporting ELL Students in Responsive ELA Classrooms (2017) Melinda J. McBee Orzulak

Writing across Culture and Language: Inclusive Strategies for Working with ELL Writers in the ELA Classroom (2017) Christina Ortmeier-Hooper

Students' Rights to Read and Write Strand

Adventurous Thinking: Fostering Students' Rights to Read and Write in Secondary ELA Classrooms (2019) Mollie V. Blackburn, editor

In the Pursuit of Justice: Students' Rights to Read and Write in Elementary School (2020) Mariana Souto-Manning, editor

In the Pursuit of Justice

Students' Rights to Read and Write in Elementary School

Edited by

Mariana Souto-Manning
Teachers College, Columbia University

National Council of Teachers of English
340 N. Neil St., Suite #104, Champaign, Illinois 61820
www.ncte.org

Staff Editor: Bonny Graham
Imprint Editor: Cathy Fleischer
Interior Design: Victoria Pohlmann
Cover Design: Pat Mayer
Cover Image: Karen Sprowal

NCTE Stock Number: 48204; eStock Number: 48211
ISBN 978-0-8141-4820-4; eISBN 978-0-8141-4821-1

Library of Congress Cataloging-in-Publication Data

Names: Souto-Manning, Mariana, editor. | National Council of Teachers of English, issuing body.
Title: In the pursuit of justice : students' rights to read and write in elementary school / edited by Mariana Souto-Manning.
Description: Champaign, Illinois : National Council of Teachers of English, [2020] | Series: Principles in practice | Includes bibliographical references and index. | Summary: "Provides vivid examples of how elementary school teachers make NCTE's position statements on students' rights to read and write and use their own languages come alive in their diverse classroom settings"—Provided by publisher.
Identifiers: LCCN 2019049211 (print) | LCCN 2019049212 (ebook) | ISBN 9780814148204 (trade paperback) | ISBN 9780814148211 (adobe pdf)
Subjects: LCSH: English language—Study and teaching (Elementary)—United States. | Language arts (Elementary)—Social aspects—United States. | Culturally relevant pedagogy—United States. | Multicultural Education—United States. | Multilingual education—United States. | Social justice and education—United States. | Right to Education—United States.
Classification: LCC LB1576 .S873 2020 (print) | LCC LB1576 (ebook) | DDC 372.6—dc23
LC record available at https://lccn.loc.gov/2019049211
LC ebook record available at https://lccn.loc.gov/2019049212

Contents

The Students' Right to Read

The NCTE Executive Committee reaffirmed this guideline in November 2012.

This statement was originally developed in 1981, revised April 2009 to adhere to NCTE's Policy on Involvement of People of Color, and revised again in September 2018.

Overview: The Students' Right to Read provides resources that can be used to help discuss and ensure students' free access to all texts. The genesis of the Students' Right to Read was an original Council statement, "Request for Reconsideration of a Work," prepared by the Committee on the Right to Read of the National Council of Teachers of English and revised by Ken Donelson. The current Students' Right to Read statement represents an updated second edition that builds on the work of Council members dedicated to ensuring students the freedom to choose to read any text and opposing "efforts of individuals or groups to limit the freedom of choice of others." Supported through references from text challenges and links to resources, this statement discusses the history and dangers of text censorship which highlight the breadth and significance of the Students' Right to Read. The statement then culminates in processes that can be followed with different stakeholders when students' reading rights are infringed.

The Right to Read and the Teacher of English

For many years, American schools have been pressured to restrict or deny students access to texts deemed objectionable by some individual or group. These pressures have mounted in recent years, and English teachers have no reason to believe they will diminish. The fight against censorship is a continuing series of skirmishes, not a pitched battle leading to a final victory over censorship.

We can safely make two statements about censorship: first, any text is potentially open to attack by someone, somewhere, sometime, for some reason; second, censorship is often arbitrary and irrational. For example, classics traditionally used in English classrooms have been accused of containing obscene, heretical, or subversive elements such as the following:

- Plato's *Republic*: "the book is un-Christian"
- Jules Verne's *Around the World in Eighty Days*: "very unfavorable to Mormons"
- Nathaniel Hawthorne's *The Scarlet Letter*: "a filthy book"
- Shakespeare's *Macbeth*: "too violent for children today"
- Fyodor Dostoevsky's *Crime and Punishment*: "a poor model for young people"
- Herman Melville's *Moby-Dick*: "contains homosexuality"

Modern works, even more than the classics, are criticized with terms such as "filthy," "un-American," "overly realistic," and "anti-war." Some books have been attacked merely for being "controversial," suggesting that for some people the purpose of education is not the investigation of ideas but rather the indoctrination of a certain set of beliefs and standards. Referencing multiple years of research completed by the American Library Association

The Students' Right to Read

(ALA), the following statements represent complaints typical of those made against modern works of literature:

- J. D. Salinger's *The Catcher in the Rye*: "profanity, lurid passages about sex, and statements defamatory to minorities, God, women, and the disabled"
- John Steinbeck's *The Grapes of Wrath*: "uses the name of God and Jesus in a vain and profane manner"
- Peter Parnell and Justin Richardson's *And Tango Makes Three*: "anti-ethnic, anti-family, homosexuality, religious viewpoint, unsuited to age group"
- Harper Lee's *To Kill a Mockingbird*: "promotes racial hatred, racial division, racial separation, and promotes white supremacy"
- Katherine Paterson's *Bridge to Terabithia*: "occult/Satanism, offensive language, violence"
- Toni Morrison's *The Bluest Eye*: "offensive language, sexually explicit, unsuited to age group"
- Jessica Herthel and Jazz Jennings's *I Am Jazz*: "inaccurate, homosexuality, sex education, religious viewpoint, and unsuited for age group"

Some groups and individuals have also raised objections to literature written specifically for young people. As long as novels intended for young people stayed at the intellectual and emotional level of *A Date for Marcy* or *A Touchdown for Thunderbird High*, censors could forego criticism. But many contemporary novels for adolescents focus on the real world of young people—drugs, premarital sex, alcoholism, divorce, gangs, school dropouts, racism, violence, and sensuality. English teachers willing to defend classics and modern literature must be prepared to give equally spirited defense to serious and worthwhile children's and young adult novels.

Literature about minoritized ethnic or racial groups remains "controversial" or "objectionable" to many adults. As long as groups such as African Americans, Pacific Islanders, American Indians, Asian Americans, and Latinxs "kept their proper place"—awarded them by a White society—censors rarely raised their voices. But attacks have increased in frequency as minoritized groups have refused to observe their assigned "place." Though nominally, the criticisms of literature about minoritized racial or ethnic groups have usually been directed at "bad language," "suggestive situations," "questionable literary merit," or "ungrammatical English" (usually oblique complaints about the different dialect or culture of a group), the underlying motive for some attacks has unquestionably been discriminatory. Typical of censors' criticisms of ethnic works are the following comments:

- Maya Angelou's *I Know Why the Caged Bird Sings*: "homosexuality, offensive language, racism, sexually explicit, unsuited to age group"
- Rudolfo Anaya's *Bless Me, Ultima*: "occult/Satanism, offensive language, religious viewpoint, sexually explicit, violence"
- Khaled Hosseini's *The Kite Runner*: "sexual violence, religious themes, 'may lead to terrorism'"

The Students' Right to Read

- Sherman Alexie's *The Absolutely True Diary of a Part-Time Indian*: "anti-family, cultural insensitivity, drugs/alcohol/smoking, gambling, offensive language, sex education, sexually explicit, unsuited for age group, violence, depictions of bullying"

Books are not alone in being subject to censorship. Magazines or newspapers used, recommended, or referred to in English classes have increasingly drawn the censor's fire. Few libraries would regard their periodical collection as worthwhile or representative without some or all of the following publications, but all of them have been the target of censors on occasion:

- *National Geographic*: "Nudity and sensationalism, especially in stories on barbaric foreign people."
- *Scholastic Magazine*: "Doctrines opposing the beliefs of the majority, socialistic programs; promotes racial unrest and contains very detailed geography of foreign countries, especially those inhabited by dark people."
- *National Observer*: "Right-wing trash with badly reported news."
- *New York Times*: "That thing should be outlawed after printing the Pentagon Papers and helping our country's enemies."

The immediate results of demands to censor books or periodicals vary. At times, school boards and administrators have supported and defended their teachers, their use of materials under fire, and the student's right of access to the materials. At other times, however, special committees have been formed to cull out "objectionable works" or "modern trash" or "controversial literature." Some teachers have been summarily reprimanded for assigning certain works, even to mature students. Others have been able to retain their positions only after initiating court action.

Not as sensational, but perhaps more important, are the long range effects of censoring the rights of educators and students to self-select what they read and engage with. Schools have removed texts from libraries and classrooms and curricula have been changed when English teachers have avoided using or recommending works which might make some members of the community uncomfortable or angry. Over the course of their schooling, many students are consequently "educated" in a system that is hostile to critical inquiry and dialogue. And many teachers and other school staff learn to emphasize their own sense of comfort and safety rather than their students' needs.

The problem of censorship does not derive solely from the small anti-intellectual, ultra-moral, or ultra-patriotic groups which will typically function in a society that guarantees freedom of speech and freedom of the press. The present concern is rather with the frequency and force of attacks by others, often people of good will and the best intentions, some from within the teaching profession. The National Council of Teachers of English, the National Education Association, the American Federation of Teachers, and the American Library Association, as well as the publishing industry and writers themselves agree: pressures for censorship are great throughout our society.

The material that follows is divided into two sections. The first on "The Right to Read" is addressed to parents and the community at large. The other section, "A Program of

The Students' Right to Read

Action," lists Council recommendations for establishing professional committees in every school to set up procedures for book selection, to work for community support, and to review complaints against texts. *Where suspicion fills the air and holds scholars in line for fear of their jobs, there can be no exercise of the free intellect. . . . A problem can no longer be pursued with impunity to its edges. Fear stalks the classroom. The teacher is no longer a stimulant to adventurous thinking; she [sic] becomes instead a pipe line for safe and sound information. A deadening dogma takes the place of free inquiry. Instruction tends to become sterile; pursuit of knowledge is discouraged; discussion often leaves off where it should begin.*

—Justice William O. Douglas, United States Supreme Court:
Adler v. Board of Education, 1951

The Right to Read

An open letter to our country from the National Council of Teachers of English:

The right to read, like all rights guaranteed or implied within our constitutional tradition, can be used wisely or foolishly. In many ways, education is an effort to improve the quality of choices open to all students. But to deny the freedom of choice in fear that it may be unwisely used is to destroy the freedom itself. For this reason, we respect the right of individuals to be selective in their own reading. But for the same reason, we oppose efforts of individuals or groups to limit the freedom of choice of others or to impose their own standards or tastes upon the community at large.

One of the foundations of a democratic society is the individual's right to read, and also the individual's right to freely choose what they would like to read. This right is based on an assumption that the educated possess judgment and understanding and can be trusted with the determination of their own actions. In effect, the reader is freed from the bonds of chance. The reader is not limited by birth, geographic location, or time, since reading allows meeting people, debating philosophies, and experiencing events far beyond the narrow confines of an individual's own existence.

In selecting texts to read by young people, English teachers consider the contribution each work may make to the education of the reader, its aesthetic value, its honesty, its readability for a particular group of students, and its appeal to young children and adolescents. English teachers, however, may use different texts for different purposes. The criteria for choosing a text to be read by an entire class are somewhat different from the criteria for choosing texts to be read by small groups.

For example, a teacher might select John Knowles's *A Separate Peace* for reading by an entire class, partly because the book has received wide critical recognition, partly because it is relatively short and will keep the attention of many slower readers, and partly because it has proved popular with many students of widely differing skill sets. The same teacher, faced with the responsibility of choosing or recommending books for several small groups of students, might select or recommend books as different as Nathaniel Hawthorne's *The Scarlet Letter*, Alexander Solzhenitsyn's *One Day in the Life of Ivan Denisovitch*, Marjane Satrapi[1]'s *Persepolis*, Malcolm X's *The Autobiography of Malcolm X*, Charles Dickens's *Great Expectations*, Carlos Bulosan's *America Is in the Heart*, or Paul Zindel's *The Pigman*, depending upon the skills and interests of the students in each group.

And the criteria for suggesting books to individuals or for recommending something worth reading for a student who casually stops by after class are different from selecting material for a class or group. As opposed to censoring, the teacher selects texts, and also helps guide students to self-select them. Selection implies that one is free to choose a text, depending upon the purpose to be achieved and the students or class in question, but a book selected this year may be ignored next year, and the reverse. Censorship implies that certain works are not open to selection, this year or any year.

Wallace Stevens once wrote, "Literature is the better part of life. To this it seems inevitably necessary to add / provided life is the better part of literature" (1957). Students and parents have the right to demand that education today keep students in touch with the reality of the world outside the classroom. Many of our best literary works ask questions as valid and significant today as when the literature first appeared, questions like "What is the nature of humanity?" "Why do people praise individuality and practice conformity?" "What do people need for a good life?" and "What is the nature of a good person?" English teachers must be free to employ books, classic or contemporary, which do not hide, or lie to the young, about the perilous but wondrous times we live in, books which talk of the fears, hopes, joys, and frustrations people experience, books about people not only as they are but as they can be. English teachers forced through the pressures of censorship to use only safe or antiseptic works are placed in the morally and intellectually untenable position of lying to their students about the nature and condition of humanity.

The teacher must exercise care to select or recommend works for class reading and group discussion. One of the most important responsibilities of the English teacher is developing rapport and respect among students. Respect for the uniqueness and potential of the individual, an important facet of the study of literature, should be emphasized in the English class. One way rapport and respect can be developed is through encouraging the students themselves to explore and engage with texts of their own selection. Also, English classes should reflect the cultural contributions of minoritized groups in the United States, just as they should acquaint students with diverse contributions by the many peoples of the world. Finally, the teacher should be prepared to support and defend their classroom and students' process in selecting and engaging with diverse texts against potential censorship and controversy.

The Threat to Education

Censorship leaves students with an inadequate and distorted picture of the ideals, values, and problems of their culture. Writers may often represent their culture, or they may stand to the side and describe and evaluate that culture. Yet partly because of censorship or the fear of censorship, many writers are ignored or inadequately represented in the public schools, and many are represented in anthologies not by their best work but by their "safest" or "least offensive" work.

The censorship pressures receiving the greatest publicity are those of small groups who protest the use of a limited number of books with some "objectionable" realistic elements, such as *Brave New World, Lord of the Flies, George, The Joy Luck Club, Catch-22, Their Eyes*

The Students' Right to Read

Were Watching God, or *A Day No Pigs Would Die*. The most obvious and immediate victims are often found among our best and most creative English teachers, those who have ventured outside the narrow boundaries of conventional texts. Ultimately, however, the real victims are the students, denied the freedom to explore ideas and pursue truth wherever and however they wish.

Great damage may be done by book committees appointed by national or local organizations to pore over anthologies, texts, library books, and paperbacks to find passages which advocate, or seem to advocate, causes or concepts or practices these organizations condemn. As a result, some publishers, sensitive to possible objections, carefully exclude sentences or selections that might conceivably offend some group, somehow, sometime, somewhere.

The Community's Responsibility

Individuals who care about the improvement of education are urged to join students, teachers, librarians, administrators, boards of education, and professional and scholarly organizations in support of the students' right to read. Widespread and informed support in and across communities can assure that

- enough residents are interested in the development and maintenance of a rigorous school system to guarantee its achievement;
- malicious gossip, ignorant rumors, internet posts, and deceptive letters to the editor will not be circulated without challenge and correction;
- news media will observe that the public sincerely desires objective reporting about education, free from slanting or editorial comment which destroys confidence in and support for schools;
- the community will not permit its resources and energies to be dissipated in conflicts created by special interest groups striving to advance their ideologies or biases; and
- faith in democratic processes will be promoted and maintained.

A Program of Action

Censorship in schools is a widespread problem. Teachers of English, librarians, and school administrators can best serve students, literature, and the profession today if they prepare now to face pressures sensibly, demonstrating on the one hand a willingness to consider the merits of any complaint and on the other the courage to defend their literacy program with intelligence and vigor. The Council therefore recommends that schools undertake the following two-step program to protect the students' right to read:

- establish a diverse committee that is representative of the local school community to consider book selection procedures and to screen complaints; and
- promote a community atmosphere in which local residents may be enlisted to support the freedom to read.

Procedures for Text Selection

Although one may defend the freedom to read without reservation as one of the hallmarks of a free society, there is no substitute for informed, professional, and qualified book selection. English teachers are typically better qualified to choose and recommend texts for their classes than persons not prepared in the field. Nevertheless, administrators have certain legal and professional responsibilities. For these reasons and as a matter of professional courtesy, they should be kept informed about the criteria and the procedures used by English teachers in selecting books and the titles of the texts used.

In each school, the English department should develop its own statement explaining why literature is taught and how books are chosen for each class. This statement should be on file with the administration before any complaints are received. The statement should also support the teacher's right to choose supplementary materials, to build a diverse classroom library, and to discuss controversial issues insofar as they are relevant. In addition, students should be allowed the right to self-select books to read from classroom and school library shelves.

Operating within such a policy, the English department should take the following steps:

- Establish a committee to support English teachers in finding exciting and challenging texts of potential value to students at a specific school. Schools without departments or small schools with a few English teachers should organize a permanent committee charged with the responsibility of alerting other teachers to new texts just published, or old texts now forgotten which might prove valuable in the literacy program. Students should be encouraged to participate in the greatest degree that their development and skill sets allow.

- Devote time at each department or grade-level meeting to reviews and comments by the above committee or plan special meetings for this purpose. Free and open discussions on texts of potential value to students would seem both reasonable and normal for any English department. Teachers should be encouraged to challenge any texts recommended or to suggest titles hitherto ignored. Require that each English teacher give a rationale for any text to be read by an entire class. Written rationales for all texts read by an entire class would serve the department well if censorship should strike. A file of rationales should serve as impressive evidence to the administration and the community that English teachers have not chosen their texts lightly or haphazardly.

- Report to the administration the texts that will be used for class reading by each English teacher.

- A procedure such as this gives each teacher the right to expect support from fellow teachers and administrators whenever someone objects to a text.

The Legal Problem

Apart from the professional and moral issues involved in censorship, there are legal matters about which NCTE cannot give advice. The Council is not a legal authority. Across the nation, moreover, conditions vary so much that no one general principle applies. In some

The Students' Right to Read

states, for example, textbooks are purchased from public funds and supplied free to students; in others, students must rent or buy their own texts.

The legal status of textbook adoption lists also varies. Some lists include only those books which must be taught and allow teachers and sometimes students the freedom to select additional titles; other lists are restrictive, containing only books which may be required for all students.

As a part of sensible preparations for handling attacks on books, each school should ascertain what laws apply to it.

Preparing the Community

To respond to complaints about texts, every school should have a committee of teachers (and possibly students, parents, and other representatives from the local community) organized to

- inform the community about text selection procedures;
- enlist the support of residents, possibly by explaining the place of literacy and relevant texts in the educational process or by discussing at meetings of parents and other community groups the texts used at that school; and
- consider any complaints against any work. No community is so small that it lacks concerned people who care about their children and the educational program of the schools, and will support English teachers in defending books when complaints are received. Unfortunately, English teachers too often are unaware or do not seek out these people and cultivate their goodwill and support before censorship strikes.

Defending the Texts

Despite the care taken to select worthwhile texts for student reading and the qualifications of teachers selecting and recommending books, occasional objections to a work will undoubtedly be made. All texts are potentially open to criticism in one or more general areas: the treatment of ideologies, of minorities, of gender identities, of love and sex; the use of language not acceptable to some people; the type of illustrations; the private life or political affiliations of the author or the illustrator.

Some attacks are made by groups or individuals frankly hostile to free inquiry and open discussion; others are made by misinformed or misguided people who, acting on emotion or rumor, simply do not understand how the texts are to be used. Others are also made by well-intentioned and conscientious people who fear that harm will come to some segment of the community if a particular text is read or recommended.

What should be done upon receipt of a complaint?

- If the complainant telephones, listen courteously and refer them to the teacher involved. That teacher should be the first person to discuss the text with the person objecting to its use.
- If the complainant is not satisfied, invite them to file the complaint in writing, but make no commitments, admissions of guilt, or threats.

- If the complainant writes, contact the teacher involved and have the teacher call the complainant.
- For any of the situations above, the teacher is advised to be aware of local contractual and policy stipulations regarding such situations, and keep a written record of what transpired during the complaint process.

An additional option is to contact the NCTE Intellectual Freedom Center to report incidents and seek further resources (http://www2.ncte.org/resources/ncte-intellectual-freedom-center/ [2]).

Request for Reconsideration of a Text

Author _____

Paperback_____ Hardcover _____ Online _____

Title _____

Publisher (if known) _____

Website URL (if applicable) _____

Request initiated by _____

Telephone _____

Address _____

City / State / Zip _____

Complainant represents

____ (Name of individual) _____

____ (Name of organization) _____

- Have you been able to discuss this work with the teacher or librarian who ordered it or who used it?
  ___ Yes ___ No
- What do you understand to be the general purpose for using this work?
- Provide support for a unit in the curriculum?
  ___ Yes ___ No
- Provide a learning experience for the reader in one kind of literature?
  ___ Yes ___ No
- Provide opportunities for students self-selected reading experiences?
  ___ Yes ___ No
- Other _____
- Did the general purpose for the use of the work, as described by the teacher or librarian, seem a suitable one to you?
  ___ Yes ___ No

If not, please explain.

_____
_____

- What do you think is the author's general purpose for this book?

_____
_____

The Students' Right to Read

- In what ways do you think a work of this nature is not suitable for the use the teacher or librarian wishes to carry out?

  _____

  _____

- What have been students' responses to this work?

  ___ Yes ___ No

  If yes, what responses did the students make?

  _____

  _____

- Have you been able to learn what qualified reviewers or other students have written about this work?

  ___ Yes ___ No

  If yes, what are those responses?

  _____

  _____

- Would you like the teacher or librarian to give you a written summary of what qualified reviewers and other students have written about this book or film?

  ___ Yes ___ No

- Do you have negative reviews of the book?

  ___ Yes ___ No

- Where were they published?

  _____

- Would you be willing to provide summaries of their views you have collected?

  ___ Yes ___ No

- How would you like your library/school to respond to this request for reconsideration?

  _____ Do not assign/lend it to my child.

  _____ Return it to the staff selection committee/department for reevaluation.

  _____ Other—Please explain

  _____

  _____

- In its place, what work would you recommend that would convey as valuable a perspective as presented in the challenged text?

  _____

  _____

Signature _____

Date_____

At first, the English teacher should politely acknowledge the complaint and explain the established procedures. The success of much censorship depends upon frightening an unprepared school or English department into some precipitous action. A standardized procedure will take the sting from the first outburst of criticism and place the burden of proof on the objector. When the reasonable objector learns that they will be given a fair hearing through

The Students' Right to Read

following the proper channels, they are more likely to be satisfied. The idle censor, on the other hand, may well be discouraged from taking further action. A number of advantages will be provided by the form, which will

- formalize the complaint,
- indicate specifically the work in question,
- identify the complainant,
- suggest how many others support the complaint,
- require the complainant to think through objections in order to make an intelligent statement on the text and complaint (1, 2, and 3),
- cause the complainant to evaluate the work for other groups than merely the one they first had in mind (4),
- establish the familiarity of the complainant with the work (5),
- give the complainant an opportunity to consider the criticism about the work and the teacher's purpose in using the work (6, 7, and 8), and
- give the complainant an opportunity to suggest alternative actions to be taken on the work (9 and 10).

The committee reviewing complaints should be available on short notice to consider the completed "Request for Reconsideration of a Work" and to call in the complainant and the teacher involved for a conference. Members of the committee should have reevaluated the work in advance of the meeting, and the group should be prepared to explain its findings. Membership of the committee should ordinarily include an administrator, the English department chair, and at least two classroom teachers of English. But the department might consider the advisability of including members from the community and the local or state NCTE affiliate. As a matter of course, recommendations from the committee would be forwarded to the superintendent, who would in turn submit them to the board of education, the legally constituted authority in the school.

Teachers and administrators should recognize that the responsibility for selecting texts for class study lies with classroom teachers and students, and that the responsibility for reevaluating any text begins with the review committee. Both teachers and administrators should refrain from discussing the objection with the complainant, the press, or community groups. Once the complaint has been filed, the authority for handling the situation must ultimately rest with the administration and school board.

Freedom of inquiry is essential to education in a democracy. To establish conditions essential for freedom, teachers and administrators need to follow procedures similar to those recommended here. Where schools resist unreasonable pressures, the cases are seldom publicized and students continue to read works as they wish. The community that entrusts students to the care of an English teacher should also trust that teacher to exercise professional judgment in selecting or recommending texts. The English teacher can be free to teach literacy, and students can be free to read whatever they wish only if informed and vigilant groups, within the profession and without, unite in resisting unfair pressures.

The Students' Right to Read

References

American Library Association (2013, March). *Banned & Challenged Classics*. http://www.ala
.org/advocacy/bbooks/frequentlychallengedbooks/classics (Accessed June 15, 2018).

American Library Association. (2018). *Top Ten Most Challenged Books Lists*. http://www.ala
.org/advocacy/bbooks/frequentlychallengedbooks/top10#Before%201990 (Accessed July
15, 2018)

American Library Association. (2018). *Top 10 Most Challenged Books of 2017: Resources &
Graphics*. http://www.ala.org/advocacy/bbooks/NLW-Top10 (Accessed July 15, 2018)

Stevens, W. (1957, April). Adagia Part One. *Poetry*, 41–44.

The Committee on the Right to Read of the National Council of Teachers of English:

- *Edward R. Gordon, Yale University, New Jersey, Chair*
- *Martin Steinmann, University of Minnesota, Associate Chair*
- *Harold B. Allen, University of Minnesota*
- *Frank A. Doggett, D. U. Fletcher High School, Jacksonville Beach, Florida*
- *Jack Fields, Great Neck South High School, New York*
- *Graham S. Frear, St. Olaf College, Minnesota*
- *Robert Gard, Camelback High School, Phoenix, Arizona*
- *Frank Ross, Detroit Public Schools, Michigan*
- *Warren Taylor, Oberlin College, Ohio*

Statement Authors

This document was revised by an NCTE working committee comprising the following:

- Benjamin "Benji" Chang, Education University of Hong Kong, Chair
- Anna Lavergne, Houston Independent School District, Texas
- Kim Pinkerton, Texas A&M University, Commerce
- Pernille Ripp, Oregon School District, Oregon, Wisconsin
- Gabe Silveri, Cypress Fairbanks Independent School District, Houston, Texas

Permission is granted to reproduce in whole or in part the material in this publication, with proper credit to the National Council of Teachers of English. Some schools may wish to modify the statements and arrange separately for printing or duplication. In such cases, of course, it should be made clear that revised statements appear under the authorization and sponsorship of the local school or association, not NCTE.

Article printed from NCTE: **http://www2.ncte.org**

URL to article: **http://www2.ncte.org/statement/righttoreadguideline/**

URLs in this post:

[1] Marjane Satrapi: **https://en.wikipedia.org/wiki/Marjane_Satrapi**

[2] http://www2.ncte.org/resources/ncte-intellectual-freedom-center/: **http://www2.ncte.org/
resources/ncte-intellectual-freedom-center/**

NCTE Beliefs about the Students' Right to Write

Approved by the NCTE Executive Committee, July 2014

During this era of high-stakes testing, technology-based instruction, and increased control over students' expression due to school violence, students' right to write must be protected. Censorship of writing not only stifles student voices but denies students important opportunities to grow as both writers and thinkers. Through the often messy process of writing, students develop strategies to help them come to understand lessons within the curriculum as well as how their language and ideas can be used to communicate, influence, reflect, explain, analyze, and create.

The National Council of Teachers of English believes

- The expression of ideas without fear of censorship is a fundamental right.
- Words are a powerful tool of expression, a means to clarify, explore, inquire, and learn as well as a way to record present moments for the benefit of future generations.
- Students need many opportunities to write for a variety of purposes and audiences in all classes. Teachers who regularly engage students in such writing should not be expected to read or grade all compositions.
- Teacher feedback should avoid indoctrination because of personal beliefs and should be respectful of both the writer and his/her ideas, even those with which the teacher disagrees.
- English language arts teachers are qualified to frame and assign student writing tasks, but students should, as much as possible, have choice and control over topics, forms, language, themes, and other aspects of their own writing while meeting course requirements.
- Teachers should avoid scripted writing that discourages individual creativity, voice, or expression of ideas.
- Teachers should engage students fully in a writing process that allows them the necessary freedom to formulate and evaluate ideas, develop voice, experiment with syntax and language, express creativity, elaborate on viewpoints, and refine arguments.
- Teachers should foster in students an understanding and appreciation of the responsibilities inherent in writing and publication by encouraging students to assume ownership of both the writing process and the final product.
- Teachers should explicitly teach the distinction between violent writing and violence in writing. Students should expect teachers to uphold the law in reporting all instances of violent writing.
- When writing for publication, students should be provided with high-quality writing instruction and be taught how to write material that is not obscene, libelous, or substantially disruptive of learning throughout the school.

NCTE Beliefs about the Students' Right to Write

- Administrators should work in collaboration with students who write for school publications such as school newspapers or literary magazines and, within the limits of state law or district/school policies, should avoid prior review.
- Districts should encourage the development and adoption of policies that support student writers as they learn to make choices in their writing that express their intent while still maintaining ethical and legal boundaries.

This position statement may be printed, copied, and disseminated without permission from NCTE.

Part I
Teaching in the Pursuit of Justice: Students' Rights to Read and Write in Elementary School

Mariana Souto-Manning
Teachers College, Columbia University

During this era of high-stakes testing . . . and increased control over students' expression . . . students' right[s] to [read and] write must be protected. Censorship of [reading and] writing not only stifles student voices but denies students important opportunities to grow as . . . [readers,] writers and thinkers.

—NCTE Beliefs about the Students' Right to Write *(2014)*

S tudents have the rights to read and write . . . from the earliest grades. Even before stringing symbols together to make meaning and decoding words written in books, young children are readers and writers in and of their worlds (Bentley & Souto-Manning, 2019; Lindfors, 2008; Souto-Manning & Yoon, 2018). They recognize the important people in their lives, they communicate their need for nourishment, and they read symbols within their homes and communities. They read their environments as texts. After all, reading goes well beyond decoding printed words.

As literate beings, young children learn to communicate—to read the world and write themselves in it—because it serves an important function (Bentley & Souto-Manning, 2019; Halliday, 1993). As such, they use gestures as actionable requests. They pick up toy telephones and pretend to talk to family members. Whether with store-bought or child-made costumes, they dress up as superheroes, firefighters, unicorns, and astronauts. Through their bodies (and embodiments), they write themselves in the world. They show us how writing is much more than marks on a page or symbols on a screen.

Although seldom regarded as such, young children arrive in our elementary school classrooms as capable literate beings. That is, they make meaning and make sense with and of symbols before ever setting foot in our classrooms. This premise undergirds our responsibilities as teachers—to uphold and defend students' rights to read and write in the elementary grades.

Young children's rights to read and write must be defended. As young children enter elementary school classrooms, teachers, employing mandated benchmark assessments, often feel pressured to disregard their sophisticated literacy practices in favor of a restrictive set of skills, which narrows what counts as literacy. From such a perspective, literacy becomes defined as simply decoding words and writing symbols (letters), which strung together make up words. But— you may be wondering—isn't this the way literacy has always been defined? No! And even if literacy *had* been defined in this way, such a reductionist definition of literacy fails to account for the literacies young children have developed throughout their earliest years—from infancy on. Let me explain.

Young children's rights to read and write.

Where Do Restrictive Notions of Literacy Come From?

Restrictive notions of literacy can be traced to dominant ideologies that "narrowly define literacy and value school-based literacy as the only authentic type" (Mahiri & Sablo, 1996, p. 164). Such ideologies construct school-based literacy "as a neutral baseline, while masking the maintenance of white privilege and domination" (Harris, 1993, p. 1715) in education writ large and literacy in particular. They are visible in policies emanating from crises produced to protect systems of exclusion and racial subjugation.

For example, the well-known report *A Nation at Risk* (National Commission on Excellence in Education, 1983), issued more than thirty years ago by the Reagan administration, declared education in the United States to be a failure. Its first sentence declared: "Our nation is at risk." This alarmist report went on to state, "If an unfriendly foreign power had attempted to impose on America the mediocre educational performance that exists today, we might well have viewed it as an act of war." Although short (thirty-six pages long), this report led to a narrowing of curriculum and a slew of testing policies to foster segregation and inequity (Kendi, 2016a, 2016b; Knoester & Au, 2017) under the stated purpose of proving that US education was not a failure. Specifically pertaining to reading, it offered a number of "indicators of risk," including the following:

- Some 23 million American adults are functionally illiterate by the simplest tests of everyday reading, writing, and comprehension.
- About 13 percent of all 17-year-olds in the United States can be considered functionally illiterate. Functional illiteracy among minority youth may run as high as 40 percent. (NCEE, 1983)

Relatedly, in the mid-1990s, under the guise of the seemingly neutral concepts of rigor and achievement (Kendi, 2016a, 2016b; Riley, 2017), the rhetoric of educational failure continued to narrow what was conceptualized and valued as reading. This happened as the Reading Excellence Act (H.R. 2614) was being signed into law in 1998 and two key reports were commissioned by expert panels authorized by the US Congress: (1) *Preventing Reading Difficulties in Young Children* (Snow, Burns, & Griffin, 1998) and (2) *Teaching Children to Read: A Report of the National Reading Panel* (National Reading Panel, 2000). Recommendations from these documents directly informed the No Child Left Behind legislation and the funding attached to its implementation (National Conference of State Legislatures, n.d.).

These examples shed light onto a long history marked by denying students of color the rights to read and write. Dominant definitions of reading and of writing, as well as the materials and structures we chiefly employ to teach reading and writing, have invariably been influenced by these developments. That is, the definition of literacy we currently employ in US elementary schools, the materials we have, and the measures we use are predominantly informed by narrow conceptualizations of literacy. As such, they are likely to suppress our students' rights to read and write—and they are unlikely to mirror our students' experiences and practices.

The Construction of Risk through Narrow Definitions of Literacy

In addition to narrowing what counts as literacy, these policies and reports (exemplified above) constructed children and youth of color as risks. They sanctioned racial, cultural, and linguistic inequities as acceptable—or, at the very least, as a logical outcome of their supposedly poor upbringing (Harris, 1993). One example of how they created a deficit narrative about children and youth of color can be seen in one of the bulleted points excerpted from *A Nation at Risk* (see p. 5). In labeling up to 40 percent of 17-year-olds of color as functionally illiterate, as opposed to 13 percent of the general population, without an explanation of the structural constraints and societal inequities framing such a "gap," the report constructed youth of color as risks. The pathological findings dispensed by these reports issued by "expert" commissions indicated that the United States was behind other nations in terms of educational achievement. Children in US schools—and their teachers—were constructed as needing help discerning which materials and programs would best address the risks identified. In other words, the narrative authored by these reports implied that, left to their own devices, teachers would continue to fail their students—and the United States would likely fall further behind.

Solutions were quickly offered to address the "crisis," which had been constructed by these (and other) reports that then informed education policy. These solutions were not devised by teachers, as members of the profession, but by outsiders who stood to profit from such a manufactured crisis—namely, publishers, curriculum developers, and test makers. Tools were soon provided under the guise that they would save US schools and boost US literacy achievement.

In uncritically responding to the recommendations issued and practices identified by these reports, commercial publishers flooded the market with reading and writing materials that did not reflect the backgrounds and experiences of many students. Thus, such reports effectively censored certain materials from classrooms and took choice away from students and teachers alike. These assessments and curriculum guides, marketed under the guise of bettering US education, served to dismember literacy—pulling away parts and decontextualizing them, as is the case of many phonics programs that do not include actual books—and to disempower children's ways of knowing. In fact, policy related to language and literacy insist[s] that children and teachers in schools and centers live with a disconnect, with this educational paradox: There is a profusion of human diversity in our schools and an astonishingly narrow offering of curricula. (Genishi & Dyson, 2009, p. 10)

This became particularly true for children from minoritized[1] backgrounds who, albeit not constituting the current numeric minority, are often treated in ways that marginalize their voices, values, experiences, and knowledges.

These narrow definitions of literacy, informed by high-stakes testing and increased administrative control of curricula, recycle "the view of children as empty vessels to be filled by behaviorist-oriented, scripted lessons" (Genishi & Dyson, 2009, p. 10). They prioritize what young children cannot do, instead of valuing, leveraging, and cultivating what they can do. This restrictive approach to literacy development has been problematically predicated on four interrelated understandings, rooted in racist ideas and entangled forms of bigotry (Kendi, 2016a; 2016b):

1. That some families provide their young children with "rich language and literacy" while others do not;

2. That children from families who provide "rich literacy and language" do better in school than those from "language poor families";

3. That "exposure to less common, more sophisticated vocabulary (i.e., rare words) at home relates directly to children's vocabulary acquisition"; and

4. That the "better" a child's vocabulary, the better reader they will be—and this depends on how their families use "sophisticated" and "rare" words in everyday conversations (Strickland, 2004, p. 87).

While there are varying perspectives on the link between vocabulary and reading as it pertains to early literacy development (e.g., Cunningham & Carroll, 2015; Davis, 2003; Gee, 1999; Sénéchal & LeFevre, 2014; Souto-Manning & Yoon, 2018; Wasik, Hindman, & Snell, 2016; Willis, 2015), I trouble the understanding that some families are "language poor" while others are "language rich" and that some families use "sophisticated vocabulary" (deemed to be better or superior) while others do not. This is especially problematic because the families who are deemed to have "language rich" practices and employ "sophisticated vocabulary" are predominantly white,[2] economically comfortable, dominant-American-English[3]-speaking (these descriptors often go unlabeled in research studies), and those who are deemed to be "language poor" are disproportionately families of color (Davis, 2003; Gee, 1999; Souto-Manning & Yoon, 2018; Willis, 2015). Further, by proposing that it is up to families to change their language and literacy practices to align with those (over)valued in schools, educators embrace assimilationist stances and disproportionately place the blame for minoritized children's schooling failure, or at least their early literacy development, on their families' communicative practices and linguistic repertoires. And by teaching children that "sophisticated vocabulary" is superior to their families' and communities' "ways with words" (Heath, 1983), we teachers (perhaps inadvertently) communicate the perceived inadequacy of, or their lack of regard for, minoritized children's families and for their very communicative practices.

To be sure, the concept of "language-poor families" furthers an ideology of pathology—the view that it is the children and not the teaching that needs to be remediated— problematically locating the issue of children's low achievement and lagging literacy skills within the family and not within the context of classrooms and schools, even as these tend to uphold dominant ways of being and behaving as norms (Goodwin, Cheruvu, & Genishi, 2008). In contrast, expansive and inclusive notions of literacy—those that uphold our students' rights to read and write (National Council of Teachers of English, 2018; NCTE, 2014)—go much beyond such narrow conceptualizations of literacy. Fundamentally, equitable and inclusive notions of literacy require us teachers to reject the "word gap" rhetoric, a rhetoric that has been troubled by many researchers over the past decade (e.g., Dudley-Marling & Lucas, 2009; Michaels, 2013). Instead, it requires us to identify, leverage, and sustain the sophisticated communicative practices and linguistic repertoires of traditionally minoritized families and communities, centering them in and through our teaching.

Equitable and inclusive notions of literacy, which are foundational to upholding our students' rights to read and write and to the pursuit of justice, require us to understand that there isn't a "gap," as purported by *A Nation at Risk* thirty-five years ago. Instead, they require us to understand that there is "a language debt owed to minoritized individuals and communities" (Souto-Manning & Yoon, 2018, p. 162), thus inviting us to revise our assumptions about accountability and answerability. Instead of holding minoritized students and their families responsible for bridging the academic gap, which is conceptualized as a problem of the individual, they urge us to position society as answerable for the language debt that has escalated cross-generationally, as African languages were stripped from enslaved Africans (Smitherman, 1998), Mexican American children were degraded in schools (Alemán & Luna, 2013), Indigenous languages were forcibly replaced by English (National Museum of the American Indian, 2007), and Asian American children were failed by schooling for not knowing English (e.g., *Lau v. Nichols*). Further, an equitable and inclusive understanding of literacy asks to consider the literacy debt, which acknowledges that enslaved Africans were denied the right to learn how to read and write by a number of "anti-literacy statutes of education restrictions" passed in twelve states by 1835 (Watson, 2009, p. W69), that the powerful oral literacies of First Nations were devalued in favor of overvaluing the written word embodied by the forces of settler colonialism (Grande, 2004), and that dominant American English was positioned as superior to languages such as Spanish and Chinese by schools and schooling, impacting the language rights of minoritized children and communities (Alemán & Luna, 2013; Wiley, 2007). Throughout American history, "rights and privileges have been distributed selectively based on the recognition of legal status" (Wiley, 2007, p. 89). Thus, chattel slavery, settler colonialism, and other forms of exclusion (challenged by legal cases at state and federal levels, such as *Hernandez v. Driscoll CISD* and *Lau v. Nichols*) effectively deny minoritized communities' rights to reading, to writing, and to their language practices.

As Delpit (1988) explained more than thirty years ago, in the United States, "Children from middle-class homes tend to do better in school than those from non-middle-class homes because the culture of the school is based on the culture of the upper and middle classes—of those in power" (p. 283). These inequities are exacerbated by societal investments (including, but not limited to, financial investments). That is, there is greater financing of curricula and materials representing dominant language and literacy practices in US society, which translates into more value being attributed to them (Souto-Manning & Martell, 2016; Souto-Manning et al., 2018).

While there is a misalignment between the practices of minoritized children, families, and communities and what is (over)valued in US schools, thus creating the false notion of failure for and by minoritized children (many of whom are children of color who speak languages other than dominant American English), it is simply inadequate to blame children and families for such misalignment or to judge their literacies and language repertoires unfavorably as a result. Such a judgment continues to perpetuate inequity in schooling and in society and compromises children's rights to read, to write, and to engage in their ways of communicating and utilize their full linguistic repertoires in our classrooms and schools (CCCC, 1974; NCTE, 2018, 2014).

Important Concepts

Chattel slavery is "the most common form of slavery known to Americans. This system, which allowed people—considered legal property—to be bought, sold and owned forever, was supported by the US and European powers in the 16th–18th centuries" (National Underground Railroad Freedom Center, 2020). Here's a resource for teaching about chattel slavery: https://www.tolerance.org/sites/default/files/2018-02/TT-Teaching-Hard-History-American-Slavery-Report-WEB-February 2018.pdf.

Settler colonialism is "the removal and erasure of Indigenous peoples in order to take the land for use by settlers in perpetuity. . . . This means that settler-colonialism is not just a vicious thing of the past, such as the gold rush, but exists as long as settlers are living on appropriated land and thus exists today" (Morris, 2019). Elementary school students must "understand that the United States couldn't exist without its settler-colonial foundation" (Morris, 2019) and acknowledge how many of us live on stolen lands. Here's a resource for teaching about settler colonialism: https://www.tolerance.org/magazine/what-is-settlercolonialism.

Important Cases

Hernandez v. Driscoll CISD (1948–1957) was a legal case that "represented the final attempt of the Texas school system to cling to its 'language' rationale in order to maintain legal segregation of Mexican Americans" (Allsup, 1982, p. 94, cited in Alemán, 2004, p. 6). It sought to interrupt the common practice of Mexican American children being grouped separately (and held back) to learn English in their public schools, even when English was their only language. This case illustrates the punishing reach of policies against speaking languages other than English. Mexican American children were degraded for speaking Spanish. In fact,

> Mexican American students were relegated to a "beginner," "low," and then "high" first grade—a practice that was not uncommon across the Southwest. School officials argued in the case that this practice was necessary because the "retardation of Latin children" would adversely impact the education of White children. (Video Project, 2020)

Such ideologies led Mexican American families to eliminate Spanish and languages other than English from their communicative repertoires as a way of protecting their children from harm. The documentary *Stolen Education* (Alemán & Luna, 2013) provides an understanding of this case. It can be accessed here: https://www.videoproject.com/Stolen-Education.html.

Lau v. Nichols (1974) was a class action lawsuit seeking to ensure the language rights of Chinese students in San Francisco United School District, a US Supreme Court case in which the Court unanimously decided that:

> The failure of the San Francisco school system to provide English language instruction to approximately 1,800 students of Chinese ancestry who do not speak English, or to provide them with other adequate instructional procedures, denies them a meaningful opportunity to participate in the public educational program and thus violates § 601 of the Civil Rights Act of 1964, which bans discrimination based "on the ground of race, color, or national origin," in "any program or activity receiving Federal financial assistance," and the implementing regulations of the Department of Health, Education, and Welfare.

This decision resulted in the Lau Remedies, which were applied to all school districts in the United States, ensuring the availability of bilingual programs, including subject matter instruction in students' home languages. Teachers can learn more about *Lau v. Nichols* by reading the ruling in the case (http://cdn.loc.gov/service/ll/usrep/usrep414/usrep414563/usrep414563.pdf) and by watching the series *Celebrate Heritage, Celebrate Unity* on YouTube, a three-part series on the history of bilingual education in the San Francisco United School District (Bartlebaugh, 2007). Students may also enjoy this YouTube video made with Powtoon: https://www.youtube.com/watch?v=Q7eUeXqGDGO.

It is important to understand that assessing language and literacy development "against dominant practices, as with studies such as the one conducted by Hart and Risley (2003)—blaming individual children, their families, and their communities for a perceived word gap"—is problematic at best (Souto-Manning & Yoon, 2018, p. 191). At the same time, it is essential to acknowledge that the pressures associated with—and offered as a solution to—the US "crisis" in education in general and in literacy in particular are very real.

We teachers are often told that children from minoritized backgrounds enter our classrooms "with no language" and that they need more vocabulary, since their family is "language poor." Without understanding the problem inherent with labels such as "language poor," it is easy—even with the best intentions—to engage in literacy practices that fail to uphold students' rights to read and write (NCTE, 2018; NCTE, 2014) and, as a result, deny students' very humanity. To suspend this harm, fully honor the humanity of the children we teach, and mobilize literacy teaching in the pursuit of justice, "[n]arrow visions need to be replaced with the complex scenes that are spacious enough for children's diverse ways of being. . . . That more welcoming terrain has space for the strengths and resources of children" of color (Genishi & Dyson, 2009, p. 10).

Thus, to defend and uphold students' rights, we must consider the language debt owed to minoritized communities. As with the "education debt" (defined by Ladson-Billings, 2006), the language debt is:

- historical—US schooling imposed assimilation, erasure, and subjugation onto people of color via communicative practices that upheld the interests of whiteness, including the overprivileging of dominant American English;
- economic—throughout history, seeking to uphold the dominance of whiteness, policymakers resourced schools marked by dominant language practices and characterized by whiteness in terms of ways of knowing, communicating, being, and behaving;
- sociopolitical—decisions that ensure the civic process is predominantly or exclusively written in dominant American English also ensure white dominance; and
- moral—in "counting the words a child speaks, the field distorts the bigger issue: how dominant languages continue to privilege dominant groups and individuals, as well as how language has served to discriminate, segregate, disempower, and dehumanize" (Souto-Manning & Yoon, 2018, p. 194).

Students' Rights to Read and Write

In light of the language debt and of restrictive notions of literacy resulting from the standardization of curriculum and teaching, the National Council of Teachers of English (NCTE), a US-based professional organization dedicated to improving

Dreaming about expansive notions of what counts as literacy.

the teaching of literacy and language at all levels, issued two important statements. These statements—*The Students' Right to Read* (2018) and *NCTE Beliefs about the Students' Right to Write* (2014)—help us teachers defend our students' literacies, cultivate their ability to make choices, and uphold their rights to read books that represent who they are and to write in ways that make sense to them, often multi-modally, challenging restrictive notions of literacy. These statements open up the definition of literacy, reclaiming student and teacher agency. They call for "students' free access to all texts" (NCTE, 2018, p. vii). (All page references to these position statements map to the texts reprinted in the front matter of this book.) As such, they serve as powerful forces, and also as rationales for teachers seeking to empower their students—and themselves—in a pressure-filled time when restrictive literacy curricula (e.g., E. D. Hirsch's Core Knowledge) and teaching practices (what some call "teaching moves"—e.g., Lemov, 2010) are widely adopted, often defining teaching as merely a technical enterprise.

The Students' Right to Read (NCTE, 2018) underscores the importance of freedom. In doing so, it acknowledges the ingrained problematics of determining which books may or may not be appropriate for students and rejects the use of prescribed materials or reading levels as tools for censoring. When teachers are "forced through the pressures of censorship to use only safe or antiseptic works," we "are placed in the morally and intellectually untenable position of lying to [our] students about the nature and condition of humanity" (NCTE, 2018, p. xi), sanctioning dominant societal values as normal or acceptable, and communicating that the views, values, practices, and experiences of minoritized communities (e.g., LGBTQ+ speakers of African American Language) are unusual or marginal. Book censorship is a simple way to marginalize children, families, and communities.

"Since the 1800s, attitudes about which books are 'appropriate' for kids to read have too often suppressed stories" portraying the historical legacies, cultural practices, language repertoires, and lived experiences of minoritized persons, families, and communities (Ringel, 2016, para. 1). We see this with books such as *And Tango Makes Three* (2005) by Justin Richardson and Peter Parnell, the story of two male penguins in the Central Park Zoo who become a family, and *The Hate U Give* (2017) by Angie Thomas, which addresses police brutality through the eyes of a Black teenager, Starr, both of which are banned in many US schools and school districts. So censoring books is a harmful practice that compromises our students' right to read—and may ultimately deny their very humanity.

Recognizing how censorship has historically silenced the voices of communities that have been and continue to be minoritized, NCTE has denounced censorship as often arbitrary and irrational. Further, in defending students' right to read, it recognizes that any work can be deemed inappropriate or unsafe for and by someone in society. *The Students' Right to Read* thus offers guidance for teachers who experience censorship of books and other reading materials (magazines, sites, newspapers, etc.). It explains:

> Literature about minoritized ethnic or racial groups remains "controversial" or "objectionable" to many adults. As long as groups such as African Americans, Pacific Islanders, American Indians, Asian Americans, and Latinxs "kept their proper place" —awarded them by a White society—censors rarely raised their voices. But attacks have increased in frequency as minoritized groups have refused to observe their assigned "place." Though nominally, the criticisms of literature about minoritized racial or ethnic groups have usually been directed at "bad language," "suggestive situations," "questionable literary merit," or "ungrammatical English" (usually oblique complaints about the different dialect or culture of a group), the underlying motive for some attacks has unquestionably been discriminatory. (2018, p. viii)

The statement denounces commonly employed comments such as "offensive language, sexually explicit, unsuited to age group" (employed in response to Toni Morrison's *The Bluest Eye*), "inaccurate, homosexuality, sex education, religious viewpoint, and unsuited for age group" (referring to Jessica Herthel and Jazz Jennings's *I Am Jazz!*), and "anti-family, homosexuality, religious viewpoint, unsuited to age group" (referring to Justin Richardson and Peter Parnell's *And Tango Makes Three*).

Although it would be easy to dismiss censorship concerns as long-ago-and-far-away, they are alive and well today. For example, in today's society we witness the police department of Charleston, South Carolina, calling for the censorship of two books, *The Hate U Give* by Angie Thomas (2017) and *All American Boys* by Jason Reynolds and Brendan Kiely (2015), both by and about Black people, because they purportedly promote "distrust of police" (Leah, 2018). As if acts of racism and police brutality hadn't been committed persistently throughout the country, resulting in the murder of too many Black lives. This call for censorship is a direct affront to the NCTE statement *The Students' Right to Read*, which states that "teachers must be free to employ books, classic or contemporary, which do not hide, or lie to the young, about the perilous but wondrous times we live in, books which talk of the fears, hopes, joys, and frustrations people experience, books about people not only as they are but as they can be" (2018, p. xi).

Far too often, censored books represent minoritized populations. For example, one of the most banned children's books of all time is *And Tango Makes Three* (2005), based on a true story of two male penguins at the Central Park Zoo who adopted an egg and hatched a baby chick, Tango, thereby forming a family. The censorship of *And Tango Makes Three* has been justified on religious grounds. This is problematic, as it disavows Rudine Sims Bishop's notion that books (and bookshelves) need to serve as windows, mirrors, *and* sliding glass doors. She explained:

> We need diverse books because we need books in which children can find themselves, see reflections of themselves. . . . Children need to see themselves reflected, but books can also be windows, so you can look through and see other worlds and see how they match up or don't match up to your own, but the sliding glass door allows you to enter that world as well, and so that's the reason why the diversity needs to go both ways. It's not just children who have been underrepresented and marginalized, but it's also the children who always find their mirrors in the books and, therefore, get an exaggerated sense of their own self-worth and a false sense of what the world is like. (Reading Rockets, 2015)

This is all the more necessary when children's books overwhelmingly portray white characters and are overwhelmingly written by white authors (Cooperative Children's Book Center, 2019). And, as NCTE affirms, literature "should reflect the cultural contributions of minoritized groups in the United States, just as they should acquaint students with diverse contributions by the many peoples of the world" (2018). Although this is easier said than done given publishing trends.

The Cooperative Children's Book Center (CCBC) at the University of Wisconsin-Madison detailed how in 2015, only 14.3 percent of children's books published in the United States were about American Indians, Latinxs, Asians and Asian Americans, and Africans and African Americans combined. In 2017 this percentage rose to 24.8 percent. While the percentage of books about people of color is rising, it still represents less than half of the actual population of schoolchildren of color, which has been more than 50 percent in the United States since 2014. And children's books published in the United States written by authors of color constituted 10.2 percent in 2015 and 14.2 percent in 2017. In light of the percentage of children of color in today's classroom (more than 50 percent nationwide), this amounts to a huge racial disproportionality.

Magazines, newspapers, and websites have, like books, come under attack, due to nudity, poorly reported news, and other reasons. Yet, as the NCTE statement on reading explicates, "One of the foundations of a democratic society is the individual's right to read, and also the individual's right to freely choose what they would like to read. This right is based on an assumption that the educated possess judgment and understanding and can be trusted with the determination of their own actions" (p. x). The statement also links the right to read to freedom:

> The right to read, like all rights guaranteed or implied within our constitutional tradition, can be used wisely or foolishly. In many ways, education is an effort to improve the quality of choices open to all students. But to deny the freedom of choice in fear that it may be unwisely used is to destroy the freedom itself. For this reason, we respect the right of individuals to be selective in their own reading. But for the same reason, we oppose efforts of individuals or groups to limit the freedom of choice of others or to impose their own standards or tastes upon the community at large. (2018, p. x)

In addition to *The Students' Right to Read*, NCTE issued a document titled *NCTE Beliefs about the Students' Right to Write* (2014), which clarifies its conviction that students have the "fundamental right" to express "ideas without fear of censorship" (p. xix). This includes, but is not limited to, expressing their ideas in ways that are different from the practices typically (over)valued in their classrooms and schools (e.g., written stories and essays in dominant American English). Going much beyond writing in the traditional sense, the statement seeks to protect students' right to author in and across multiple named languages. To uphold students' rights, the statement specifically rejects reductive notions of literacy, affirming: "Teachers should avoid scripted writing that discourages individual creativity, voice, or expression of ideas" (p. xix). Instead, teachers need to offer students many opportunities, materials, and modes for authoring "for a variety of purposes and audiences," employing an array of communicative practices and linguistic repertoires.

In alignment with the CCCC/NCTE *Students' Right to Their Own Language* statement (adopted in 1972 and published in a special issue of *College Composi-*

tion and Communication in 1974), *NCTE Beliefs about the Students' Right to Write* (2014) affirms students' right to "their own patterns and varieties of language—the dialect of their nurture or whatever dialects in which they find their own identity and style" (Conference on College Composition and Communication, 1974). Thus, upholding students' right to write requires rejecting "the myth of a standard American dialect" (CCCC, 1974), questioning its very validity, and acknowledging that the language of power is the language of "those who have power" (Delpit, 1988, p. 282). It requires work on our part as teachers, interrupting and unlearning prevalent myths in schooling and society.

For example, despite the "myth of a standard American dialect" (CCCC, 1974) or of a standard language (what some refer to as "standard English"), speakers of languages other than dominant American English continue to be seen and positioned in many settings as less capable than speakers of dominant American English. Fifth-grade teacher Alice Lee recalls thinking of African American Language (AAL) as "slang," and asking, "Aren't we doing a disservice by allowing [students] . . . to talk like that in the classroom, when they are expected to speak in standard English in the real world?" (2017, p. 27). This ingrained and pervasive myth prevails today. Challenging such myths leads to learning (about African American language *as* a language, for example) and to understanding that "'correcting' African American language speakers is counterproductive" (p. 27), harmful, and damaging; it compromises students' right to write—and their very humanity. As teachers we must commit to engaging our "students fully in a writing process that allows them the necessary freedom to formulate and evaluate ideas, develop voice, experiment with syntax and language, express creativity, elaborate on viewpoints, and refine arguments" (NCTE, 2014, p. xix), and this includes the use of communicative practices and linguistic repertoires with which we ourselves may not be familiar or that may push back against what is regarded as "academic language." After all, words are powerful and freedom matters.

Regarding words as a "powerful tool of expression, a means to clarify, explore, inquire, and learn as well as a way to record present moments for the benefit of future generations," the *NCTE Beliefs about the Students' Right to Write* (2014, p. xix) requires us teachers to work with our students in ways that honor their ways with words, the power of their words, instead of engaging in teaching that promotes processes of assimilation and linguistic erasure. It urges us to sustain students' voices and stories, to honor their rich legacies and sophisticated communicative practices—even if and when they are not part of the "official" literacy curriculum—asking us to "avoid indoctrination" and to "be respectful of both the writer and his/her ideas, even those with which the teacher disagrees" or is unfamiliar. This requires us to be committed to envisioning and enacting pedagogies that are not filtered through a lens of contempt and pity (e.g., the "achievement gap") but, rather, are centered on contending in complex ways with the rich and innovative linguistic, literate, and cultural practices of . . . communities of color. (Paris and Alim, 2014, p. 86)

Defending and upholding our students' right to write is predicated on supporting our students' diverse and rich cultural practices and sophisticated—albeit often silenced—communicative repertoires. This should be apparent in our mindset as well as visible in our teaching practice (Souto-Manning et al., 2018).

But the NCTE statement not only identifies teachers' responsibilities in upholding students' right to write (and author, broadly conceived), but it also identifies the responsibilities of administrators and school districts, stating that they "should work in collaboration with students who write for school publications . . . and, within the limits of state law or district/school policies, should avoid prior review" (2014, p. xx). This can be a difficult stance—yet it is one that cannot be compromised, even within an ever-growing climate of hyper-surveillance. Although censorship within the context of elementary schools does not often make it into the news, in the very school where some of the teachers who are contributors to this book teach or have taught, PS 75 in New York City, a visual literacy project authored by students in a kindergarten came under attack after it was critiqued by conservative commentator Sean Hannity and resulted in "a deluge of threatening phone calls, profanity-laden emails and violent social media posts after conservative bloggers published an article calling a student-made fundraising project an example of left-wing indoctrination" (McKay, 2016). Although the administrator's response was critiqued in vicious and problematic ways, it *was* the administrator's responsibility to uphold students' right to author, even from the earliest elementary school years. Doing so reaffirms students' capabilities and protects their rights—as learners, as writers, and as individuals.

The statements issued by NCTE not only seek to protect students' rights to read and write, but also serve as much-needed reminders that these are *rights*, not privileges to be dispensed as rewards or in ways that foster disproportionality. This is a point I take up in the conclusion of this book (Chapter 9) as I frame the rights to read and write as human rights. After all, antiliteracy movements and laws have been in place historically to dispossess, disempower, and dehumanize individuals and communities of color (e.g., Davis, 1981; Walker, 2009; Fisher, 2009).

But before we situate these rights within a history of antiliteracy laws, we turn to how they come to life within the context of today's elementary classrooms. Drawing on the NCTE position statements *The Students' Right to Read* and *NCTE Beliefs about Students' Right to Write*, Part II of this book unveils the ways in which eight New York City public school teachers engaged with the principles identified in these statements through their everyday practice. To do so, they critically problematized and interrupted approaches to reading, writing, and talk that do not prioritize students' rights, teaching in ways that honored the full humanity of their students, in the pursuit of justice.

Prioritizing Students' Rights to Read and Write in the Classroom

In the chapters that constitute Part II: In The Classroom, eight elementary public school teachers link their classroom practices to concepts described in these NCTE position statements, thereby defining students' rights in elementary school classrooms as they pertain to reading, writing, and talk. Part II consists of six vignettes written in first-person voice by elementary school teachers who have engaged in teaching and/or designed learning experiences that foster students' rights to read and to write in their own languages in their classrooms. All of these teachers currently work in New York City public schools. They teach grades 1 through 5 and work with students representing diverse demographics. They themselves are diverse in terms of race, ethnicity, income, gender identity, language practices, and sexuality. They share an assets view of the communities their students come from, a clear belief in the brilliance of the children they teach, a commitment to fostering critical multicultural competence (positioning themselves and their students as change agents), and literacy teaching practices that seek to problematize injustices and foster critical consciousness (Gorski, 2009; Ladson-Billings, 1995; Souto-Manning & Martell, 2016; Souto-Manning et al., 2018).

Here, I briefly introduce the focus of each of their vignettes:

- In "Students' Right to Representation in the Early Childhood Curriculum," second-grade teacher Carmen Lugo Llerena denounces how while stories matter, they are disproportionately Eurocentric and thus do not represent the majority of students in today's US classrooms. Through classroom examples, Carmen shares how she presents students with counternarratives to the prescribed curricular text.

- In "Students' Right to Author Their Identities," fourth-grade teacher Alison Lanza offers windows into her hip-hop-education-informed practices in second and fourth grades (Emdin, 2016). Firm in her belief that students have the right to learn about who they are, Alison shares how she uses hip-hop as a framework to design learning experiences that help her students interrupt and dismantle injustice.

- In "Students' Rights to Their Names, Languages, and Cultures," fourth-grade dual language special education teacher Benelly Álvarez explains how—despite time pressures and curricular mandates—she committed to reading books by and about Latinx individuals and communities (reflective of her student population). She then explores visual autobiographies as sites for her students to acknowledge and reflect on their identities and identify their rich cultural and historical legacies.

- In "'Learning is mostly about English': Students' Right to Trouble the Language of Power," teachers Emma Pelosi and Patty Pión discuss how they interrupted students' perceptions of language hierarchies within the context of a second-grade dual language classroom. Exploring immigration, chattel slavery, discrimination, and patriotism through open-ended questions and student-led inquiries, they fostered student choice and cultivated agency and voice.

- In "Students' Rights to Read and Write about Homophobia and Hate Crimes," fourth/fifth-grade coteachers Jessica Martell and Billy Fong discuss how they engaged the class with the 2016 mass shooting at the Pulse nightclub in Orlando, Florida. They share their concerns and discomfort approaching this topic and explain how they resolved those issues and designed activities that fostered students' reading and writing development and allowed them to explore social injustice.

- In "Students' Right to Trauma-Informed Literacy Teaching," first-grade teacher Karina Malik explains how she strives to cultivate a trauma-informed classroom. She specifically shares how she begins the year by creating an environment of trust and transparency and then builds a supportive environment that empowers students' voices and stories—orally and in writing.

Grounded in firm commitments to racial justice, linguistic pluralism, and cultural diversity, the chapters that make up Part II of this book focus on what grades 1–5 teachers have done to defend their students' rights to read and write—as well as their right to representation in and through reading and writing. As you will see, such representation takes many forms: their identities, their experiences, their languaging practices. As you turn the page and enter diverse New York City public school classrooms, I hope that you will be inspired to reimagine or to extend your own practice, reinventing the commitments and ideas presented in ways that are significant to your own context.

Notes

1. I use the term *minoritized* because the commonly used term *minority* is often numerically inaccurate within a context where children and youth of color constitute the numeric majority in US public schools. Further, the term *minoritized* accounts for the way in which children of color, their families, and communities are often treated as the minority, even when they are not. I borrow this term from Teresa McCarty (2002).

2. Throughout the book, when *Black* and *Brown* are used as descriptions of race, they are capitalized. When *white* is used to describe race, it is not. This seeming inconsistency is deliberate and takes a stand against the long history of white supremacy in the United States.

3. What some may call "standard English."

References

Alemán, E. Jr. (2004). *Mexican American school leadership in South Texas: Toward a critical race analysis of school finance policy.* [Unpublished doctoral dissertation]. University of Texas at Austin. Retrieved from https://repositories.lib.utexas.edu/bitstream/handle/2152/1125/alemane516920.pdf

Alemán, E. Jr., & Luna, R. (Producers), & Luna, R. (Director). (2013). *Stolen education* [Motion picture]. United States: Video Project.

Bartlebaugh, R. (2007). SFUSD bilingual education Lau vs Nichols SFGTV San Francisco. *YouTube.* Retrieved from https://www.youtube.com/watch?v=cXhQrJ37gFE

Bentley, D. F., & Souto-Manning, M. (2019). *Pre–K stories: Playing with authorship and integrating curriculum in early childhood.* New York, NY: Teachers College Press.

Conference on College Composition and Communication. (1974). Students' right to their own language. *College Composition and Communication, 25*(3). Retrieved from https://prod-ncte-cdn.azureedge.net/nctefiles/groups/cccc/newsrtol.pdf

Cooperative Children's Book Center, University of Wisconsin-Madison (CCBC). (2019). *Publishing statistics on children's/YA books about people of color and first/native nations and by people of color and first/native nations authors and illustrators.* Retrieved from https://ccbc.education.wisc.edu/books/pcstats.asp

Cunningham, A., & Carroll, J. M. (2015). Early predictors of phonological and morphological awareness and the link with reading: Evidence from children with different patterns of early deficit. *Applied Psycholinguistics, 36*(3), 509–31.

Davis, A. Y. (1981). *Women, race & class.* New York, NY: Random House.

Davis, J. E. (2003). Early schooling and academic achievement of African American males. *Urban Education, 38*(5), 515–37.

Delpit, L. D. (1988). The silenced dialogue: Power and pedagogy in educating other people's children. *Harvard Educational Review, 58*(3) 280–98.

Douglas, W. O., & Supreme Court of the United States. (1974). *U.S. Reports: Lau v. Nichols, 414 U.S. 563.* [Periodical]. Retrieved from the Library of Congress, https://www.loc.gov/item/usrep414563/

Dudley-Marling, C., and Lucas, K. (2009). Pathologizing the language and culture of poor children. *Language Arts, 86*(5), 362–70.

Emdin, C. (2016). *For White folks who teach in the hood . . . and the rest of y'all too: Reality pedagogy and urban education.* Boston, MA: Beacon Press.

Fisher, M. T. (2009). *Black literate lives: Historical and contemporary perspectives.* New York, NY: Routledge.

Gee, J. (1999). Reading versus reading something: A critique of the National Academy of Sciences' report on reading. *Yearbook of the American Reading Forum, 19,* 1–10.

Genishi, C., & Dyson, A. H. (2009). *Children, language, and literacy: Diverse learners in diverse times.* New York, NY, and Washington, DC: Teachers College Press and the National Association for the Education of Young Children.

Goodwin, A. L., Cheruvu, R., & Genishi, C. (2008). Responding to multiple diversities in early childhood education: How far have we come? In C. Genishi & A. L. Goodwin (Eds.), *Diversities in early childhood education: Rethinking and doing* (pp. 3–10). New York, NY: Routledge.

Gorski, P. C. (2009). What we're teaching teachers: An analysis of multicultural teacher education coursework syllabi. *Teaching and Teacher Education, 25*(2), 309–18.

Grande, S. (2004). *Red pedagogy: Native American social and political thought*. Lanham, MD: Rowman & Littlefield.

Halliday, M. A. K. (1993). Towards a language-based theory of learning. *Linguistics and Education, 5*, 93–116.

Harris, C. I. (1993). Whiteness as property. *Harvard Law Review, 106*(8), 1707–91.

Hart, B., & Risley, T. R. (2003). The early catastrophe: The 30 million word gap. *American Educator, 27*(1), 4–9.

Heath, S. B. (1983). *Ways with words: Language, life, and work in communities and classrooms*. New York, NY: Cambridge University Press.

Herthel, J., & Jennings, J. (2014). *I Am Jazz!* New York, NY: Dial Books for Young Readers.

Kendi, I. X. (2016a). *Stamped from the beginning: The definitive history of racist ideas in America*. New York, NY: Nation Books.

Kendi, I. X. (2016b, October 20). Why the academic achievement gap is a racist idea. *Black Perspectives*. Retrieved from https://www.aaihs.org/why-the-academic-achievement-gap-is-a-racist-idea/

Knoester, M., & Au, W. (2017). Standardized testing and school segregation: Like tinder for fire? *Race, Ethnicity and Education, 20*(1), 1–14.

Ladson-Billings, G. (1995). But that's just good teaching! The case for culturally relevant pedagogy. *Theory Into Practice, 34*(3), 159–65.

Ladson-Billings, G. (2006). From the achievement gap to the education debt: Understanding achievement in US schools. *Educational Researcher, 35*(7), 3–12.

Lau v. Nichols, 414 U.S. 563 (1974). supreme.justia.com/cases/federal/us/414/563

Leah, R. (2018, July 11). South Carolina cops vs. "The Hate U Give": Police challenge books over police brutality content. *Salon*. Retrieved from https://www.salon.com/2018/07/11/south-carolina-cops-vs-the-hate-u-give-police-challenge-books-over-police-brutality-content/

Lee, A. (2017). Why "correcting" African American language speakers is counterproductive. *Language Arts Journal of Michigan, 32*(2), 27–33.

Lemov, D. (2010). *Teach like a champion: 49 techniques that put students on the path to college*. San Francisco, CA: Jossey-Bass.

Lindfors, J. W. (2008). *Children's language: Connecting reading, writing, and talk*. New York, NY: Teachers College Press.

Mahiri, J., & Sablo, S. (1996). Writing for their lives: The non-school literacy of California's urban African American youth. *The Journal of Negro Education, 65*(2), 164–80.

McCarty, T. L. (2002). *A place to be Navajo: Rough Rock and the struggle for self-determination in Indigenous schooling*. New York, NY: Routledge.

McKay, T. (2016, March 5). A New York public school is being threatened and harassed over this art project. *Mic*. Retrieved from https://mic.com/articles/137133/a-new-york-public-school-is-being-threatened-and-harassed-over-this-art-project#.lAq6QlNvP

Michaels, S. (2013). Commentary: Déjà vu all over again: What's wrong with Hart & Risley and a "linguistic deficit" framework in early childhood education? *LEARNing Landscapes, 7*(1), 23–41.

Morris, A. (2019, January 22). What is settler-colonialism? *Teaching Tolerance*. Retrieved from https://www.tolerance.org/magazine/what-is-settlercolonialism

Morrison, T. (2007). *The bluest eye*. New York, NY: Vintage International.

National Commission on Excellence in Education (NCEE). (1983). *A nation at risk: The imperative for educational reform*. Washington, DC: The National Commission on Excellence in Education. Retrieved from https://www2.ed.gov/pubs/NatAtRisk/index.html

National Conference of State Legislatures (NCSL). (n.d.). *Literacy & No Child Left Behind (NCLB)*. Retrieved from http://www.ncsl.org/research/education/literacy-no-child-left-behind.aspx

National Council of Teachers of English. (2014). *NCTE beliefs about the students' right to write*. Retrieved from http://www2.ncte.org/statement/students-right-to-write/

National Council of Teachers of English. (2018). *The students' right to read*. Retrieved from http://www2.ncte.org/statement/righttoreadguideline/

The National Museum of the American Indian. (2007). *Native words, native warriors*. Retrieved from https://americanindian.si.edu/education/codetalkers/html/

National Reading Panel. (2000). *Teaching children to read: An evidence-based assessment of the scientific research literature on reading and its implications for reading instruction*. Retrieved from https://www1.nichd.nih.gov/publications/pubs/nrp/Documents/report.pdf

National Underground Railroad Freedom Center. (2020). *Modern abolition: Learn about five forms of slavery*. Retrieved from https://freedomcenter.org/enabling-freedom/five-forms-of-slavery

Paris, D., and Alim, H. S. (2014). What are we seeking to sustain through culturally sustaining pedagogy? A loving critique forward. *Harvard Educational Review, 84*(1), 85–100.

Reading Excellence Act, H.R. 2614, 105th Cong. (1998). Retrieved from https://www.congress.gov/bill/105th-congress/house-bill/2614

Reading Rockets. (2015, January 30). *Mirrors, windows and sliding doors* [Video file]. Retrieved from https://www.youtube.com/watch?v=_AAu58SNSyc

Reynolds, J., & Kiely, B. (2015). *All American boys: A novel*. New York, NY: Atheneum Books for Young Readers.

Richardson, J., & Parnell, P. (2005). *And Tango makes three*. New York, NY: Simon & Schuster Books for Young Readers.

Riley, D. (2017). Rigor/Us: Building boundaries and disciplining diversity with standards of merit. *Engineering Studies, 9*(3), 249–65.

Ringel, P. (2016, October 1). How banning books marginalizes children. *The Atlantic*. Retrieved from https://www.theatlantic.com/entertainment/archive/2016/10/how-banned-books-marginalize-children/502424/

Sénéchal, M., & LeFevre, J. (2014). Continuity and change in the home literacy environment as predictors of growth in vocabulary and reading. *Child Development, 85*(4), 1552–68.

Smitherman, G. (1998). Word from the hood: The lexicon of African-American vernacular English. In S. S. Mufwene, J. R. Rickford, G. Bailey, & J. Baugh (Eds.), *African-American English: Structure, history, and use* (pp. 203–25). Abingdon, UK: Routledge.

Snow, C. E., Burns, M. S., & Griffin, P. (Eds.). (1998). *Preventing reading difficulties in young children*. Washington, DC: National Academy Press. Retrieved from https://files.eric.ed.gov/fulltext/ED416465.pdf?ref=driverlayer.com/web

Souto-Manning, M., Llerena, C. L., Martell, J., Maguire, A. S., & Arce-Boardman, A. (2018*). No more culturally irrelevant teaching*. Portsmouth, NH: Heinemann.

Souto-Manning, M., & Martell, J. (2016). *Reading, writing, and talk: Inclusive teaching strategies for diverse learners, K–2*. New York, NY: Teachers College Press.

Souto-Manning, M., & Yoon, H. S. (2018). *Rethinking early literacies: Reading and rewriting worlds*. Abingdon, UK: Routledge.

Strickland, D. (2004). The role of literacy in early childhood education: Working with families as partners in early literacy. *The Reading Teacher, 58*(1), 86–88.

Thomas, A. (2017). *The hate u give*. New York, NY: Balzer + Bray/HarperCollins.

Video Project. (2020). *Stolen education* [Trailer]. Video Project. Retrieved from https://www.videoproject.com/Stolen-Education.html

Walker, V. S. (2009). Foreword. In M. T. Fisher, *Black literate lives: Historical and contemporary perspectives* (pp. xv–xix). New York, NY: Routledge.

Wasik, B. A., Hindman, A. H., & Snell, E. K. (2016). Book reading and vocabulary development: A systematic review. *Early Childhood Research Quarterly, 37*(4), 39–57.

Watson, S. E. (2009). "Good will come of this evil": Enslaved teachers and the transatlantic politics of early Black literacy. *College Composition and Communication, 61*(1), W66–W89.

Wiley, T. G. (2007). Accessing language rights in education: A brief history of the US context. In O. García & C. Baker (Eds.), *Bilingual education: An introductory reader* (pp. 89–107). Buffalo, NY: Multilingual Matters.

Willis, A. I. (2015). Literacy and race: Access, equity, and freedom. *Literacy Research: Theory, Method, and Practice, 64*(1), 23–55.

Part II
In the
Classroom

Students' Right to Representation in the Early Childhood Curriculum

Carmen Lugo Llerena
New York City Department of Education

S tories are significant. Stories of lived experiences across diverse cultures are significant. Stories crafted from children's imagination and their understandings of how the world works are significant. Yet published children's stories are disproportionately Eurocentric, reflecting a tendency to interpret the world according to European-dominant values and experiences and centering Whiteness.

Sadly, although data from the US Census Bureau indicates a continuous rise in the number of students of color across the country, publishing rates do not reflect this growth. That is, in 2018, while US public schools predominantly comprised students of color, less than one-fourth of children's books published represented their images, experiences, families, and communities. Simply put, there is a disproportionality between the fact that "white students are now the minority in U.S. public schools" (Chen, 2019) and the overwhelming whiteness of children's books being published; see Figure 1.1, an infographic developed by Sarah Park Dahlen and David Huyck.

Figure 1.1. Diversity in children's books, 2018.

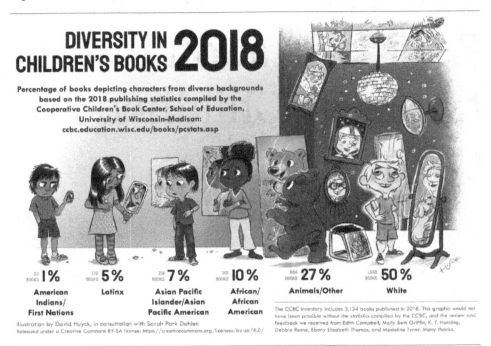

As the National Council of Teachers of English (NCTE) *Resolution on the Need for Diverse Children's and Young Adult Books* (2015) explains, the "texts that are accessible to youth are determined and authorized by influential individuals and professional organizations: editors/publishers, agents, authors/book creators, illustrators, distributors, booksellers, librarians, educators, parents, and the media." These individuals and organizations continue to overprivilege Eurocentrism. This fact is particularly disheartening, considering that more than 50 percent of students enrolled in US public schools are children of color (National Center for Educational Statistics, 2016).

According to NCTE, "In the world of literature for young people, the . . . absence of human, cultural, linguistic, and family diversity in children's and young adult literature attests to the growing disparity and inequity in the publishing history in the United States" (2015). As a result, all too often elementary school teachers are confronted with the dilemma of either following prescribed Eurocentric curricula or providing minoritized children with mirrors that reflect their own realities, windows to access multiple perspectives, and sliding glass doors to develop cultural competence (Bishop, 1990; Ladson-Billings, 1995). This last item, sliding glass doors, is necessary so that children can understand and live diversity as the norm (Genishi & Dyson, 2009). Sadly, also all too often, elementary school teachers are not aware of the whitewashing of curricula and the Eurocentricity of books in their classroom libraries. This is problematic because, as Rudine Sims Bishop, professor emerita of education at Ohio State University explained, "It's not just children who have been underrepresented and marginalized who need these books; it's also the children who always find their mirrors in the books and therefore get an exaggerated sense of their own self-worth and a false sense of what the world is like" (Reading Rockets, 2015).

In this chapter, I share how we—my coteacher Nick and I—upheld students' rights to read and write in our inclusive second-grade classroom (serving children with and without IEPs). In addition to upholding students' choice to select what they read, as identified in *The Students' Right to Read* (NCTE, 2018), we believed in expanding choice—what was available to be read and who was represented in those readings. In doing so, we recognized the right to read books representative of the demographic diversity of US society as a basic right to a democratic society (NCTE, 2018).

Nick and I fulfilled the objectives and met the standards outlined in our prescribed Eurocentric curriculum while also presenting our students with counternarratives to the prescribed curricular text and providing spaces where they could construct their own counternarratives. For instance, we were required to read fairy tales as retold by the Brothers Grimm and Hans Christian Andersen, per the Core Knowledge curriculum. Core Knowledge, authored by E. D. Hirsch, has been identified as one of the "more neoconservative solutions for raising standards by teaching 'core' knowledge to all" (Ellis & McNicholl, 2015, p. 17). As Souto-Manning and Yoon (2018) underscore, Hirsch's problematic curriculum suggests that "a single American identity needs to replace the multiplicity of cultural identities" (p. 24) of students like the ones I teach. However, seeking to uphold our students' rights to read and listen to stories representative of diversities, we also read fairy tale versions that reflected our students' cultures, such as a Mexican version of *Hansel and Gretel*, an Albanian version of *Snow White*, and an African version of *Beauty and the Beast*.

When we were required to engage with a restrictive set of tall tales that reified problematic stereotypes through American Wild West or European settings and mostly white characters, we wrote our own tall tales set in places like New York City and Puerto Rico. We did so because these places represented where our students came from, and thus such stories spoke to them. We honored our students' right to write, rooted in the NCTE belief that "through the often messy process of writing, students develop strategies to help them come to understand lessons within the curriculum as well as how their language and ideas can be used to communicate, influence, reflect, explain, analyze, and create" (2014). As a result, our collectively authored tall tale portrayed larger than life characters who looked like us and whose interests mirrored our interests, values, and experiences. In the narrative that follows, I invite you into our classroom to see how we put all this into practice.

The Eurocentric Curriculum

Fairy tales and tall tales were the first "domain" (or unit) in our second-grade reading curriculum. The domain's objectives were aligned with the state-mandated Grade 2 Common Core Reading Standards for Literature. The fairy tales and tall tales in the curriculum were read from a read-aloud anthology that also served as the teacher's guide. Per instructions for teachers, students were to be presented several images on the SMART Board to go along with the reading. The domain's fairy tale anthology showcased the "classic" versions of *The Fisherman and His Wife*, *The Emperor's New Clothes*, and *Beauty and the Beast*, based on those retold by the Brothers Grimm and Hans Christian Andersen.

The Counternarrative

Our intention was to immerse our students in a plethora of multicultural, multimedia versions of fairy tales and guide them in the process of constructing their own counternarratives. We sought out texts not only in which characters and settings reflected our minoritized students' experiences and cultures, but also by authors who were members of minoritized communities themselves. Our hope was to provide engaging and relatable mentor texts in various media, to adopt less traditional and more inclusive ways of assessing understanding of these texts, and to create purposeful and joyful learning spaces.

Once a week throughout this unit, we dedicated the English language arts periods to rotating our students through four workstations we called the *Media Center*, the *Artists Studio*, the *Actors Studio*, and the *Writers Studio*. We were fortunate to have the collaboration of Haeny Yoon, assistant professor of early childhood education at Teachers College, who was conducting research in our classroom, to plan and implement these stations. In addition, our preservice teacher helped support our students while they worked at their assigned stations.

The Media Center

The Media Center provided students access to culturally relevant fairy tales via three different sources: videos of *Happily Ever After: Fairy Tales for Every Child*, an

HBO animated series of fairy tales with multicultural settings and diverse characters; ebooks from the fairy tale collection on Epic!, a digital library for children; and dozens of picture books retelling classic fairy tales from multiple perspectives and settings (see Figure 1.2). These books included titles such as:

Abadeha: The Philippine Cinderella (2014) by Myrna J. de la Paz

Adelita: A Mexican Cinderella Story (2002) by Tomie dePaola

Brothers of the Knight (1999) by Debbie Allen

The Dragon Prince: A Chinese Beauty & the Beast Tale (1997) by Laurence Yep

The Ghanaian Goldilocks (2014) by Tamara Pizzoli

Goldy Luck and the Three Pandas (2014) by Natasha Yim

Hansel and Gretel (2009) by Rachel Isadora

The Little Red Fort (2018) by Brenda Maier

Lon Po Po: A Red-Riding Hood Story from China (1996) by Ed Young

Maiden & Princess (2019) by Daniel Haack and Isabel Galupo

Pretty Salma: A Little Red Riding Hood Story from Africa (2007) by Niki Daly

Prince & Knight (2018) by Daniel Haack

Princess and the Peas (2017) by Rachel Himes

The Princess and the Warrior: A Tale of Two Volcanoes (2016) by Duncan Tonatiuh

Rapunzel (2008) by Rachel Isadora

The Rough-Face Girl (1992) by Rafe Martin

Seriously, Cinderella Is So Annoying! The Story of Cinderella as Told by the Wicked Stepmother (2012) by Trisha Speed Shaskan

The Stinky Cheese Man and Other Fairly Stupid Tales (2007) by Jon Scieszka

The Three Little Javelinas (2011) by Susan Lowell

The Three Little Tamales (2015) by Eric A. Kimmel

Trust Me, Jack's Beanstalk Stinks! The Story of Jack and the Beanstalk as Told by the Giant (2012) by Eric Braun

Students were invited to utilize all three sources and were tasked with completing a graphic organizer to demonstrate understanding of every story they viewed or read. In doing so, not only were they developing their reading comprehension skills, but they were also expanding their understanding of fairy tales beyond the traditional Eurocentric canon.

Figure 1.2. The Media Center.

The Artists Studio: Creating Puppets

In the Artists Studio (see Figure 1.3), students were given an assortment of arts and crafts materials and were tasked with creating puppets that represented their interpretation of at least one of the characters in (1) *Snow White Stories around the World: 4 Beloved Tales* (2015) by Jessica Gunderson, (2) *The Fisherman and His Wife* (2008) by Rachel Isadora, or (3) *Truly, We Both Loved Beauty Dearly! The Story of Sleeping Beauty as Told by the Good and Bad Fairies* (2014) by Trisha Speed Shaskan, all multicultural and fractured fairy tales we read aloud in class. Fractured fairy tales, for those not familiar with this genre, are retellings of familiar stories that have been reauthored and changed in ways that include current social issues and/ or elicit laughter due to surprising and unexpected characterizations, plot developments, or oppositional perspectives or points of view (as compared to the original fairy tale). Students were also asked to share with the class their process of deciding which character to portray, their choice of materials, and what they were trying to convey about the character.

Figure 1.3. The Artists Studio.

The Actors Studio

In the Actors Studio, we sought to foster a space where students could engage in authoring multimodally. In such a space, students brought to life the hilarious tales they concocted and the dynamic characters they imagined. They drew not only on their family and community cultural knowledges, but also on their peer cultures (Souto-Manning & Yoon, 2018). For example, using *Little Red Hot* (2015) by Eric A. Kimmel as a mentor text and influenced by many other fractured fairy tales and tall tales they read throughout this unit of study, students devised their own versions of the classic *Little Red Riding Hood* and acted them out for their peers. They collaboratively wrote scripts, negotiated the casting of roles, and selected costumes and props to use during their performances. Moving beyond traditional conceptualizations of authorship that equate authoring strictly with writing, thereby disempowering some children, our students were able to author through performance. These performances were video-recorded and shared with parents and members of our school community. Thus, they served an authentic communicative purpose while also honoring children's multiple ways of making meaning in and of the world. Following is an excerpt from the transcript of one of their performances. Figure 1.4 combines the cover of the mentor text and a photograph of the children's performance.

Little Red Hot, a Popping Señor Lobo, and Pecos Bill

Little Red Hot: "What big teeth you got grandma."

Señor Lobo as Grandma: "That's to . . ."

Little Red Hot: "Wait, I know this one. To eat them big popcorns!"

Little Red Hot opens Señor Lobo's mouth and puts big popcorns in it.

Narrator: "And Señor Lobo shot right into the sky! And just a minute later,
    Pecos Bill came down the street riding his horse."

Pecos Bill: "Whatcha got there?"

Figure 1.4. The Actors Studio.

The Writers Studio

Seeking to uphold students' right to write (NCTE, 2014), we set up the Writers Studio. Our students were excited to participate in the Writers Studio even before they knew what was expected of them. Their enthusiasm was fueled by the materials presented to them, materials to which they had not previously had access for "writing in school." Each student received a 7" × 10" notebook made out of afforestation tree paper, with cream-colored pages and 6mm ruled lines (see Figure 1.5). The covers of our students' new writers notebooks, unlike the black-and-white marble cover composition notebooks to which they were accustomed, were of a light brown, cardstock-like material. Students were thrilled to customize their notebook covers with drawings and cutouts. In addition, they were provided with different sizes and colors of sticky notepads to jot down ideas and easily keep safe in their notebooks. Students who did not wish to write in their writers notebook had access to white or colored pieces of lined and unlined paper. We encouraged

Figure 1.5. The Writers Studio.

them to use writing tools other than standard graphite pencils. Students were eager to write with bright colored pens, markers, and colored pencils.

In the Writers Studio, our students were asked to write their very own fairy tales. During the prewriting stage of the writing process, they were tasked with completing a graphic organizer that helped to develop the main character of their stories. They were also encouraged to brainstorm ideas with a partner and provide each other with feedback. The Writers Studio produced many magical, action-packed kids' pop-culture-flavored tales, such as "Emma's World" and "Money NY NY," with fierce and eclectic characters and the wackiest, if not the happiest, of ever-afters.

How Counternarratives Serve as Sites to Uphold Students' Rights to Read and Write

The four curricular activities identified in this chapter allowed students to negotiate counternarratives to the traditional Eurocentric narratives privileged in the official literacy curriculum, Core Knowledge. By providing spaces for students to read and write counternarratives—versions of traditional narratives featuring characters of color and non-Eurocentric settings—alongside the texts prescribed in our Eurocentric curriculum, we were able to create a learning environment that was mindfully structured to nurture inclusivity and advance social justice in our classroom, thereby upholding students' rights to read and write. This led to more meaningful learning experiences for our students. They read across texts, comparing and contrasting multiple texts, and multimodally adapted and authored "classics" in their own context. In addition to making the curriculum more inclusive and our students' learning experiences more significant, we were able to share with other teachers the powerful outcomes achieved, even according to traditional measures of student achievement, explaining the power and possibility of providing children with an array of meaningful and authentic reading and writing opportunities to fracture traditional Eurocentric tales, agentively and critically. Our students asked critical questions of texts, such as "Who told this story?" and "Why don't the characters look like us?" Best of all, while upholding their rights to read and write texts that served as mirrors, windows, and sliding glass doors (Bishop, 1990), we fostered learning that was engaging, relatable, and fun!

References

Bishop, R. S. (1990). Mirrors, windows, and sliding glass doors. *Perspectives, 6*(3), ix–xi. Retrieved from https://scenicregional.org/wp-content/uploads/2017/08/Mirrors-Windows-and-Sliding-Glass-Doors.pdf

Chen, G. (2019, October 14). White students are now the minority in U.S. public schools. *Public School Review*. Retrieved from https://www.publicschoolreview.com/blog/white-students-are-now-the-minority-in-u-s-public-schools

Dahlen, S. P., & Huyck, D. (2019, June 19). *Picture this: Diversity in children's books 2018 infographic* [Blog post]. Retrieved from https://readingspark.wordpress.com/2019/06/19/picture-this-diversity-in-childrens-books-2018-infographic/

Ellis, V., & McNicholl, J. (2015). *Transforming teacher education: Reconfiguring the academic work*. London, UK: Bloomsbury Academic.

Genishi, C., and Dyson, A. H. (2009). *Children, language, and literacy: Diverse learners in diverse times*. New York, NY: Teachers College Press.

Ladson-Billings, G. (1995). But that's just good teaching! The case for culturally relevant pedagogy. *Theory Into Practice, 34*(3), 159–65.

National Center for Education Statistics. (2016). Table 203.50: Enrollment and percentage distribution of enrollment in public elementary and secondary schools, by race/ethnicity and region: Selected years, fall 1995 through fall 2026. *Digest of Education Statistics*. Retrieved from https://nces.ed.gov/programs/digest/d16/tables/dt16_203.50.asp

National Council of Teachers of English. (2014). *NCTE beliefs about the students' right to write*. Retrieved from http://www2.ncte.org/statement/students-right-to-write/

National Council of Teachers of English. (2018). *The students' right to read*. Retrieved from http://www2.ncte.org/statement/righttoreadguideline/

National Council of Teachers of English. (2015). *Resolution on the need for diverse children's and young adult books*. Retrieved from http://www2.ncte.org/statement/diverse-books/

Reading Rockets. (2015, January 30). *Mirrors, windows and sliding glass doors* [Video file]. Retrieved from https://www.youtube.com/watch?v=_AAu58SNSyc

Souto-Manning, M., & Yoon, H. S. (2018). *Rethinking early literacies: Reading and rewriting worlds*. Abingdon, UK: Routledge.

Children's Books

Allen, D. (1999). *Brothers of the knight* (K. Nelson, Illus.). New York, NY: Dial Books for Young Readers.

Braun, E. (2012). *Trust me, Jack's beanstalk stinks! The story of Jack and the beanstalk as told by the giant* (C. Bernardini, Illus.). North Mankato, MN: Picture Window Books.

Daly, N. (2007). *Pretty Salma: A Little Red Riding Hood story from Africa*. New York, NY: Clarion Books.

de la Paz, M. (2014). *Abadeha: The Philippine Cinderella* (Y. Tang, Illus.). New York, NY: Shen's Books.

dePaola, T. (2002). *Adelita*. New York, NY: G. P. Putnam's Sons.

Gunderson, J. (2015). *Snow White stories around the world: 4 beloved tales* (C. Madden, Illus.). North Mankato, MN: Picture Window Books.

Haack, D. (2018). *Prince & knight* (S. Lewis, Illus.). New York, NY: Little Bee Books.

Haack, D., & Galupo, I. (2019). *Maiden & princess* (B. Human, Illus.). New York, NY: Little Bee Books.

Himes, R. (2017). *Princess and the peas*. Watertown, MA: Charlesbridge.

Isadora, R. (2008). *The fisherman and his wife*. New York, NY: G. P. Putnam's Sons.

Isadora, R. (2008). *Rapunzel*. New York, NY: Penguin Young Readers.

Isadora, R. (2009). *Hansel and Gretel*. New York, NY: G. P. Putnam's Sons.

Isadora, R. (2009). *The princess and the pea*. New York, NY: Puffin Books.

Kimmel, E. A. (2015). *Little Red Hot* (L. Huliska-Beith, Illus.). New York, NY: Scholastic.

Kimmel, E. A. (2015). *The three little tamales* (V. Docampo, Illus.). New York, NY: Scholastic.

Lowell, S. (2011). *The three little javelinas* (J. Harris, Illus.). Flagstaff, AZ: Rising Moon.

Maier, B. (2018). *The little red fort* (S. Sánchez, Illus.). New York, NY: Scholastic Press.

Martin, R. (1992). *The rough-face girl* (D. Shannon, Illus.). New York, NY: G. P. Putnam's Sons.

Pizzoli, T. (2014). *The Ghanaian Goldilocks* (P. Howell, Illus.). The English Schoolhouse.

Scieszka, J. (2007). *The stinky cheese man and other fairly stupid tales* (L. Smith, Illus.). New York, NY: Viking.

Shaskan, T. S. (2012). *Seriously, Cinderella is so annoying! The story of Cinderella as told by the wicked stepmother* (G. Guerlais, Illus.). North Mankato, MN: Picture Window Books.

Shaskan, T. S. (2014). *Truly, we both loved Beauty dearly! The story of Sleeping Beauty, as told by the good and bad fairies* (A. Tayal, Illus.). North Mankato, MN: Picture Window Books.

Tonatiuh, D. (2016). *The princess and the warrior: A tale of two volcanoes*. New York, NY: Abrams Books for Young Readers.

Yep, L. (1997). *The dragon prince: A Chinese Beauty & the beast tale* (K. Mak, Illus.). New York, NY: HarperCollins.

Yim, N. (2014). *Goldy Luck and the three pandas* (G. Zong, Illus.). Watertown, MA: Charlesbridge.

Young, E. (1996). *Lon Po Po: A Red-Riding Hood story from China*. New York, NY: Philomel Books.

Students' Right to Author Their Identities

Chapter Two

Alison Lanza
Central Park East II Elementary School
New York, NY

Students have the rights to learn about who they are and where their genius lies. Hip-hop can serve as a way for them to do so (Emdin, 2016). I see it as my responsibility as a teacher to uphold my students' rights to their own identities, recognizing their power. Yet I often find that by the time kids get to my second-grade or fourth-grade classroom (I share examples of both in this chapter), they have already been told who they are . . . or rather, who they aren't, or won't be, or can't become. So my main objective each year is to help children trouble reductive notions of their possible futures. I do this by helping them explore multiple perspectives.

When kids can walk away from our time together understanding the concept of empathy while also understanding their own power, I consider that a complete win. For this to happen, I must design learning experiences that help them interrupt and dismantle multiple levels of self-hate that have been—even at ages six and seven—societally imposed and learned. I do so by designing spaces for them to author their identities within the context of our classroom community. These spaces allow me to build "rapport and respect among students," an essential component described in *The Students' Right to Read* (NCTE, 2018). They are spaces where children's uniqueness is respected and their power and potential are emphasized.

In this chapter, I describe two sites for learning that afforded my students the right to author their own identities in powerful ways. The first site was my second-grade classroom a couple of years ago. The second site is my fourth-grade classroom, where I still teach. I share these sites for learning not as definitive solutions or how-tos. Instead, I hope that they serve as windows into spaces of possibility, spaces where children can reclaim and author powerful identities in other classrooms. In each of these sites, where knowledge is cogenerated and learning is codesigned (Emdin, 2016), I am both teacher and learner and my students are learners and teachers (Freire, 1998). But to begin, I explain how hip-hop education (or hip-hop ed) informs who I am and my practice as a teacher.

Alison Lanza.

Hip-Hop Ed

"Yeah, Nah"

Everybody in m.g.m.t. never wanted to believe
That hip-hop could retrieve
Math and Li-ter-a-cy
But take a walk down the hall
There it is
416
Spread love "Ayo fam, tell us your hope and dream!"
. . . What's your plan?
. . . Will you make it?
Challenge what you hear
cause this world is for the taking
The tribe cyphers up
There's good juju in the building
Kids all got a lot to say
Ideas bouncin' off the ceiling
Walking by—you may judge
Question rigor
We won't budge
But look deeper
Mask off
Social studying's a go
Finding rhythm from within
Because the kids got to know
They are seeds
They will grow
They will reap
What they sow
. . . If you can, drop your fear
Lose the guilt
Save the tears
Plan for them—not for me
Then sit back and you'll see
The most rigorous and relevant pedagogy
Shinin' light on the culture
H-I-P H-O-P
Giving kids a fuller version of their identity

(To experience the full effect of this lyrical content, play Big Daddy Kane's "Ain't No Half-Steppin'" instrumental beat.)

The above prose, authored by me, is an example of tapping into my own story through an art medium that is culturally relevant (Ladson-Billings, 1995) to the students in my classroom and to me: hip-hop. The four elements of hip-hop—deejaying, emceeing, b-boying/breaking, and graffiti (Chang, 2005)—are present in so many aspects of the classroom communities in which I have taught.

Chris Emdin (2013) redefines these elements as the pillars of hip-hop education. In classrooms and schools, he explains:

> Emceeing . . . underscores the importance of having a space for voice and performance. B-boying shows the educator that every class should have some space for movement. Graffiti emphasizes the need for showcasing student work and allowing a space for art. Dee-jaying shows us that it is necessary to allow youth to have access to engage with and manipulate technology . . . [and knowledge]. The consideration of [this as] an alternative model for teaching that introduces and validates the culture of marginalized youth (however simplistic it initially appears) stands in direct opposition to the pedagogy of poverty. (p. 94)

Let me briefly explain how these four elements of hip-hop (Chang, 2005) became pillars foundational to my practice as a hip-hop educator, shaping what goes on in the classroom. Luckily, I do not have to abide by a restrictive standardized curriculum; I teach in a progressive public school in East Harlem. But I believe that unless we reimagine education, we are doomed to enact what Emdin (2013) calls a "pedagogy of poverty," a pedagogy that impoverishes our students and compromises their futures.

As a teacher, I engage in deejaying, remixing the official curriculum with knowledges and interests children bring with them to the classroom, extending it to fully include who children are—their identities—and to account for their priorities. This entails blurring the line between home and school and co-creating a space with the learners in the room that allows voice and choice. And it is a large task. The key to beginning this work is becoming self-aware—understanding your *own* identity. Who are you and how are you seen? And if you're a white teacher, like me, who teaches learners who don't look like you, then understand that you must unpack your privilege and how it impacts your learners.

I also emcee; this means that I engage in the kind of poetry that denounces issues of inequity, especially those directly experienced by our class, its members, and the larger community to which we belong. Over time, my students emcee as well, finding a positive outlet in denouncing and working through injustices poetically. This means that we read our world, but we do not accept it uncritically. Instead, we reauthor it poetically. We name and question its injustices. We develop critical consciousness (Ladson-Billings, 1995).

As members of a classroom community who are also unique individuals, we dance to our beat at times. To be sure, we all b-boy/break dance in our own ways, moving and expressing our emotions in ways that capture our spirits. We also gather often "in a circle, and have some type of communal exchange with each other" (Emdin, 2013, p. 89). In these spaces, there is constant teaching and learning; it is

> where the novice b-boy (the peripheral participant) is being trained by the expert through the enactment of a set of practices that involve one person performing, and another person observing, emulating, and then being coached on what was previously performed. (p. 89)

We all "end up deeply engaged in the process; . . . all who are involved seem to temporarily escape reality as they commune under hip-hop" (p. 89).

To outsiders, b-boying/breaking can be a bit daunting, as it may appear chaotic. Yet, in our classroom, b-boying/breaking is a safe space where students can express their emotions in beautiful and unique ways. Our only b-boy/break dance rule is safety—students have to keep themselves, our classroom, and their peers emotionally and physically safe. In this space, my students have "choice and control over topics, forms, language, themes, and other aspects" of their learning as a right (NCTE, 2014).

Kids want to know who they are and how they're seen. Their identities may be buried under layers of distrust and uncertainty, but modeling vulnerability and relinquishing power by asking students for guidance in a field they are experts in helps to co-create a true community, a place and people worth trusting.

Finally, there is graffiti. While we do have real graffiti on our classroom wall as well as pictures of graffiti visible in our East Harlem community, the concept of graffiti allows the inclusion of multiple voices, images, and perspectives in our classroom. It also allows us to fully explore the importance of authorship through the study and action of tagging (Souto-Manning & Yoon, 2018). After all, we should all be given credit for our words and contributions to the world.

Through hip-hop ed, the classroom communities I have been part of as a teacher and a learner have built, destroyed, and rebuilt our identities through self-awareness and self-love. We have understood that our genius lies in our authenticity. We are the most connected and lit beings when we lean into what makes us, us. This requires the simultaneous focus on recognizing and honoring our roots while also discovering and growing our wings—being both past and future oriented.

Roots and wings: the overall objective each year for my teaching practice. Having children honor their roots and their cultural identity by simply holding up a mirror and letting them see their reflection as powerful creates a sense of courage and the fortitude to use their metaphorical wings to take risks and persevere in this short life. Hip-hop changes how people are seen and heard. It resonates with people who feel misrepresented and unheard. It resonates with the voiceless and the choiceless. The genre itself was birthed from an attempt to burn down the Bronx. And as a queer, hip-hop head, Catholic girl from the Bronx, one thing I know for sure is that from death comes resurrection, and from the ashes the phoenix rises.

Hip-hop education is about handing your kids the mic, listening to their voices, and co-creating curriculum, teaching, and learning. It is about positioning ourselves as learners. It is also about witnessing how children learn about and honor their roots (what Ladson-Billings [1995] calls *cultural competence*) and discover their wings. There are so many stories waiting to be told and so many scripts that need to be flipped and reclaimed.

Looking Like Me: Authoring Self in Second Grade

Assuming the role of teacher as deejay, I engaged my second-grade classroom in a read-aloud of *Looking Like Me* by Walter Dean Myers and illustrated by Christopher Myers, thinking aloud and making visible all the different ways the main character, Jeremy, is authored by his community—as a dancer, a brother, a son, etc. In response to the read-aloud, I invited my students to emcee, independently writing about themselves—to process how they were authored within and across communities and settings, denouncing oppressions. That is, I invited them to look in a metaphorical mirror and write labels that described what they saw. I also asked them to write down labels that identified how others saw them, warning them, "Some might be painful, you know?" Within the context of a whole-class meeting, I modeled what I invited them to do by writing on the easel some of the labels that described me—from my perspective and from the perspective of others. As I did so, I acknowledged how this might be a hard and painful process; some people see us for what we cannot do and for what we are not.

After modeling what I expected them to do, I sent my students to their tables, asking them to open their journals and write down labels that could be, or were, used to describe who they are. Although students were quick to get started, they soon slowed down. Writing down labels that had dehumanized them was a painful process, and as a result this activity took much longer than I had initially expected. It also required more support. Students weren't sure, for example, whether they could write words such as *gay* and *fat* when they had been used in derogatory manners to hurt. I assured them that they could write such terms down and that we would discuss them the following day.

The next day, after students had written down the labels, within the context of a whole-class community meeting we engaged in sharing our responses and making connections. This sharing offered many opportunities to assess kids' levels of, and experiences with, self-love and self-hate. We then made a mural in our classroom where the children displayed their self-love labels openly and framed a drawing of their profiles and the self-hate (or other-hating) labels crumpled up. We talked, for example, about how the word *gay* is not necessarily bad, as it can be used to describe individuals and communities in positive ways, yet it can also be used in derogatory and disrespectful ways, as had been the experience of one of their classmates. I said, "Yo, you saw one of my good labels was "gay" yesterday. Now somebody tells me it's bad. What's up with that?" This opened up a much needed conversation about homophobia and related forms of bigotry as expressed by words. "Words are powerful," I reminded my students.

I intentionally sought to foster meaningful writing and to "avoid scripted writing that discourages individual creativity, voice, or expression of ideas" (NCTE, 2014). Although *Looking Like Me* served as an invitation, all I told students was that they were to serve as their peers' metaphorical mirror, highlighting what they saw and valued about their classmates. I modeled a letter during class meeting that described my coteacher, Naomi. Then I paired them up and gave them paper to write their letters.

Later on I followed up with "unlikely pairs." I paired two kids who don't usually link up, or who maybe hold opposite perspectives or roles within our community, thus remixing our classroom community. They each had to write about the other, knowing the other would read their writing. I told them that their letters would be read by their peer, and that hopefully we would have time to share with the class during our classroom community meetings.

This process allowed students not only to process the ways in which they were authored, but also to critically (re)author one another within the context of the classroom community. Because they were aware of how each one of them had experienced being hurt by labels (as a result of the learning activity in which I asked them to label themselves), they were careful not to hurt each other with words. Students recognized that although words are just words, negative labels had real emotional consequences.

After listening to how their peers described one another, students expressed how powerful it was to hear how someone in their own "tribe" (Emdin, 2016) sees them. Here, for example, is a section of the letter Damián wrote to Omar:

> You are unique in a different way. Your heritege is speacial. Your imagination is strong even if you don't think that. So belive you can change the world and it will happen. (transcribed as written)

Students' letters to each other were powerful. As they read and listened to the letters written about them and about their peers, they said things like: "I was relieved to know I was accepted," "I didn't know that people thought that about me," and "I felt seen and heard."

The Best Part of Me: Hair as Identity

In fourth grade, we engaged as a class with the tenets of hip-hop and in rich dialogue, leveling many different stereotypes, shifting perspectives, and reclaiming our identities. We read Wendy Ewald's *The Best Part of Me: Children Talk about Their Bodies in Pictures and Words* (2002), in which children in third through fifth grades in North Carolina present descriptions and portraits of the best part of themselves, such as their nose, mouth, feet, hair. Then, in our fourth-grade classroom in a public school in East Harlem, we engaged in emceeing facets of our physical identities.

We specifically identified parts of our body that we had been teased about or that led others to try to diminish us. Then we troubled the notions of beauty at the root of such teasing and criticism—after which we remixed those critiques, denouncing inequities, and authored our own poems. In these poems, we reclaimed our identities and authored positive portrayals of our physical features. Here is one of the poems authored and emceed by a fourth grader:

My Hair . . . My Pride

I care a lot about my hair
My hair is my family
My hair is my color
And my color is my race.
And my race is who I am
My hair is like milk and cookies
It can be soft or crunchy
My hair is like a wild rose bush
Once it gets tangled
You can't undo it
I can straighten my hair
But not all the way
But that's ok
I didn't want to anyway

It must be mentioned that this poem was authored by a girl who carries herself with a quiet strength. She doesn't speak often, but when she does every child stops to pull up a seat. She's one of the pupil prophets. This child has been through more difficult traumas in her short nine years than most people go through in a lifetime. Hip-hop speaks to her, but she didn't fully realize that until her fourth-grade year.

Before she began reading her rhyme, this student turned to another classmate for an assist. She sought out the loud, boisterous pencil tapper for a beat because being the quiet girl allowed her to be a keen observer, one who was aware of the strengths of her classroom community and its members. She said, "Give me something like 'Freedom,'" referring to the Pharrell song, part of our chorus repertoire. Next thing you know, there was a staccato beat generated by the tapping of a pencil, while another student simultaneously created the bass line with his forearms and hands on the wooden table. She waited and watched like someone waiting to find her rhythm and cadence in the double-dutch ropes as they repeatedly turn. Eventually, she jumped in and created "ear art," as her classmates referred to it. Not only did she author and perform a poem, but she also reclaimed her identity positively. She no longer had "bad hair," as she had heard too many times. Her hair was "like milk and cookies" and could be "soft or crunchy." Comparing her hair to "a wild rose bush," she explained that once tangled, one "can't undo it."

As soon as they finished, a quiet and charming red-haired white boy in the class spontaneously and passionately blurted out, "Yo, that was so beautiful." None of us knew exactly which element of the poem spoke to him, but a collective head nod and a new view of that "quiet girl"—and of the annoying loud pencil tapper—seemed to create a tangible acceptance . . . and fostered community. Along with a new view of Afros as "a wild rose bush."

Reflecting on Students' Rights

Students have the rights to author their own identities in my classroom. I regard being seen and heard as essential work. This is important regardless of age, but it can and should be the work of teachers of young kids. As a teacher committed, through hip-hop ed, to upholding students' right to be who they are, I see myself simply as the outlet for these young people to plug in to in order to see their light. I hope other teachers will too.

References

Chang, J. (2005). *Can't stop, won't stop: A history of the hip-hop generation.* New York, NY: Picador.

Emdin, C. (2013). Pursuing the pedagogical potential of the pillars of hip-hop through sciencemindness. *International Journal of Critical Pedagogy, 4*(3), 83–99.

Emdin, C. (2016). *For white folks who teach in the hood . . . and the rest of y'all too: Reality pedagogy and urban education.* Boston, MA: Beacon Press.

Freire, P. (1998). *Teachers as cultural workers: Letters to those who dare teach*. Boulder, CO: Westview Press.

Ladson-Billings, G. (1995). But that's just good teaching! The case for culturally relevant pedagogy. *Theory Into Practice, 34*(3), 159–65.

National Council of Teachers of English. (2014). *NCTE beliefs about the students' right to write*. Retrieved from http://www2.ncte.org/statement/students-right-to-write/

National Council of Teachers of English. (2018). *The students' right to read*. Retrieved from http://www2.ncte.org/statement/righttoreadguideline/

Souto-Manning, M., & Yoon, H. S. (2018). *Rethinking early literacies: Reading and rewriting worlds*. Abingdon, UK: Routledge.

Children's Books

Ewald, W. (2002). *The best part of me: Children talk about their bodies in pictures and words*. Boston, MA: Little, Brown Books for Young Readers.

Myers, W. D. (2009). *Looking like me* (C. Myers, Illus.). New York, NY: Egmont.

Students' Rights to Their Names, Languages, and Cultures

Benelly Álvarez
PS 75–The Emily Dickinson School
New York, NY

This is my twelfth year working in a New York City public elementary school. Despite my years of experience as a teacher, at times it has felt as though it's my first year of teaching all over again. With a new curriculum one year and another the next, I found myself hoping that the latest one would work just right. I often recited a line from one of Celia Cruz's famous songs, "*Ríe, llora . . . a cada cual le llega su hora.*"[1] But every time I did, I wanted to cry—not because I wasn't trying my hardest, but because I felt like I wasn't getting anywhere as a teacher committed to supporting my students' learning and to cultivating their brilliance. Yet, in light of seemingly unending time pressures, I rationalized learning about and focusing on the implementation of the latest curriculum.

Looking back, I now realize that I've spent part of my teaching career learning new curricula and techniques without fully considering the faces that look back at me in the classroom. Instead of centering the children I taught—along with their rich experiences, cultural legacies, and language practices—I centered some new curriculum guide or program that dictated what I should cover. Many of these curriculum guides I dedicated time to learning about and implementing in my teaching did not seem to educate, but instead served to assimilate my students, most of whom were bilingual and multilingual students of color. With this realization, I started considering how I might begin to more fully consider my students' identities and experiences, even in light of all the time and content pressures I faced every day.

I must admit that a huge part of my teaching and my own growth as a teacher occurred in situations where a problem arose and, in a split second, I decided to address what had just happened instead of simply moving on to the next thing on the schedule. Although I am ashamed to admit it, at times I *did* move on to what was next, feeling the time pressures associated with covering content.

Not having enough time as a teacher feels like my biggest enemy. However, the experiences I share in this chapter reveal how the best work and learning comes from questions and comments that arise organically after reading books that represent my students' languages, cultural practices, and identities—not from covering boxed curriculum content like clockwork. These spontaneous questions and comments can foster deeper learning. They allow for personal connections, which are sometimes brushed off because of time pressures. They can humanize teaching and learning.

Through intentionally centering my students and prioritizing their development, instead of seeking to cover what's outlined by the latest curriculum guide, I have learned the power and necessity of going beyond the mandated curriculum. In this chapter, I recount learning events that occurred when I purposefully turned away from the mandated curriculum and created the space for my students to dig deeper into exploring and understanding their identities. My students soon learned the value of these spaces—where their rights as learners, readers, and writers were valued and protected; where they had choice, felt capable, and engaged in meaningful learning. Although intentional, these learning journeys started with one of us (whether students or teacher) vulnerably asking questions about issues of fairness and unfairness or sharing feelings of being inadequate, of not being "good enough."

Exploring Our Identities

In my dual language (Spanish-English) fourth-grade classroom, my students have the opportunity to develop and learn academic content in two languages. They typically begin the program in kindergarten and continue through fifth grade with the goal of developing as bilingual and biliterate members of society. They come from Spanish-speaking, English-speaking, bilingual, and multilingual backgrounds.

My students and I typically read two texts written in Spanish—*Me Llamo María Isabel* (1993) and *Nacer Bailando* (2011), both by Alma Flor Ada—to help us begin to ask questions about our identities and the role of language and culture in shaping who we are. These books are by and about Latinxs.[2] Although we read these books in Spanish, the English translations are always available to all the students in the classroom.

In alignment with *The Students' Right to Read* position statement, when selecting books I carefully consider who the author is, whose perspectives are centered, how these perspectives reflect the experiences of my students, and "the contribution which each work may make to the education of the reader, its aesthetic value, its honesty, its readability for a particular group of students, and its appeal" (NCTE, 2018, p. x).

Within a dual language setting, it is essential to explore issues of identity. After all, language and cultural practices are part of one's identity. These texts open the doors to discussions of identity, culture, and the role of language in our lives. They represent issues students are navigating, such as the language hierarchies society too often imposes in our lives. Additionally, they offer students opportunities to talk about themselves in ways that the mandated Eurocentric[3] curriculum does not allow.

Each year, students are empowered when they find the space to discuss their likes and dislikes, their comforts and discomforts, and their overall frustrations with "the way things just are" in society. They are also empowered when they see the injustices they experience in everyday life reflected in the literature they are reading. As Bishop (1990) underscored, such books serve as mirrors and allow us to "see our own lives and experiences as part of the larger human experience. Reading, then, becomes a means of self-affirmation" (p. ix).

In *Me Llamo María Isabel* by Alma Flor Ada, third grader María Isabel relocates to a new school and her teacher decides to call her "Mary" instead of "María Isabel," alleging that there are too many Marías in the classroom already: "We already have two Marías in this class. Why don't we call you Mary instead?" (Ada, 1993, p. 8). María Isabel experiences both isolation and frustration as the name that belongs to her, that is tied to her Puerto Rican roots, is replaced by the name Mary. María Isabel describes in detail how her names came from her grandmothers. After reading the book, my students engage in discussions that emphasize and delve into the histories of their own first and last names. This allows them not only to engage in primary source research (meeting mandated learning standards), but also to discuss their values and their families' naming practices, and to make connections between their experiences and those of the book's main character.

"My name is spelled with a *Y* and not a *J*. I don't like it when people think it's spelled the regular way," said Yessica. Another student, while pointing to the accent above the *e* in his name, expressed how he did not like the way it was being pronounced without the accent. "I don't like it when people say my name as *Caesar* when it's *César*."

I always share my own personal history by revealing to my students that my first name is not a Dominican name, although my family is Dominican, but actually an Italian last name, Benelli, with the *i* changed to *y*, and that it is often mispronounced. In some way, reading the words authored by Alma Flor Ada within the contexts we inhabit affords a space where many of us share a sense of not belonging because our names are mispronounced or changed to fit whatever the speaker is most comfortable saying. These experiences make my students and me feel as though our identities are being devalued and that we are being marginalized, "otherized," treated as "different."

Additionally, students who navigate within and across languages daily often make powerful connections to Margie, the main character in *Nacer Bailando* (2011) by Alma Flor Ada, who struggles to accept her Mexican culture and does not like to speak Spanish. After reading the book and making connections between our lives and Margie's, we vulnerably share feelings that are similar to Margie's. Opening up the space for these discussions about cultural practices and language repertoires helps all of us critically think about *why* Margie might feel the way she does and how *we* might feel about and identify with her feelings (of not wanting to speak Spanish) as well. And even though I do not feel ashamed of my language and my culture as an adult, I share with my students about times when I was younger when I had feelings and engaged in actions that were aligned with Margie's.

I personally share my own struggles growing up as a first-generation Dominican American Latina who has an Italian name and spoke only Spanish at home, and whose parents spoke Spanish but not English. The children I teach have experienced similar struggles, which they share. "My mom only speaks Spanish too," said one student, while another student said, "My mom speaks Spanish but my dad only speaks English." My experience resonates with many of my students. Together we discuss many reasons why this may be the case, and we help one another develop pride in our identities, honoring the powerful cultural legacies and language practices of our families from an asset-based perspective: not as "not knowing English," but as "Spanish speakers."

Again and again, opening up about my own identity formation allows us to create the space to ask critical questions and for critical consciousness to develop (Ladson-Billings, 1995; Souto-Manning, 2010). In such spaces, as a classroom community we explore the power of speaking multiple languages and the importance of the Spanish language in books, in our classroom, and in society. Making ourselves vulnerable (Freire, 1998), we—teacher and students alike—share how sometimes we feel shame in speaking a language other than English. At the heart of our discussions are questions such as:

- Why is that?
- What does society tell us about speaking in a language other than English?
- How do we feel about that?

We continually discuss questions such as "Is it a problem to speak Spanish?" and "What do we do when we are questioned about the language we are speaking and why we are speaking it?" These questions lead to discussions about languaging choice and the need to take ownership of our identities as bilinguals and multilinguals. This process allows us to foster a classroom where Spanish is valued and language hierarchies are questioned.

It is important to note that the work of exploring identities my students and I engage in doesn't occur within a compartmentalized block of time, nor is it included in commercially produced and district-adopted curriculum guides. It requires seeing myself as curriculum maker—with students and for students. It requires negotiating feelings of uncertainty and fighting the pseudo-sureness of the official curriculum and its pacing guides.

For me, the ability to engage in this kind of work started to develop slowly and peripherally, as I worked to find and allow pockets of time in the beginning of the day, right before lunch, when we finished a task, or when we had an open period. To be honest, even now these are the times when I start to engage my students in this type of work. I often feel unsure at first. Yet, as I witness my students' engagement, their academic, social, and emotional development—and when the focus becomes my students and not the curriculum nor my schedule—I begin to rationalize: "If standards are being met, then I can be flexible."

If I can justify why going off-script is important, I shouldn't be afraid, right? But to be completely honest, I often am. But this fear cannot get in the way of my students' brilliance. I cannot ask them to take risks if I don't take risks myself. And as I take risks, I see them growing more confident in their ability to learn and in the ways they communicate who they are and what they've learned. For example, in discussing books that matter to them, that reflect their identities and practices, students are better able to make inferences and summarize, noting how these are actually part of mandated learning standards. So, while I acknowledge the (almost always present) feeling of unsureness, my students' growth and development year after year assure me that the risk is not only worth it, but it is necessary if they are to be supported to develop fully—if their potential is to be realized.

From Reading to Visual Autobiographies

Holding several discussions about books and life often leads our class to work on visual autobiographies, or Identity Collages, which help students reflect on their own identities, their cultural practices, and historical legacies. Students are excited to engage in a different type of literacy—visual literacy—to express their identities and (re)present how they see themselves, rather than how others see them.

First and foremost, my students are just excited to do something that isn't "traditional reading and writing," although they utilize skills that develop their literacies and align with the mandated learning standards. Second, the collage allows my students to acknowledge their backgrounds and to create a space where they can publicly share their identities, establishing a sense of pride and ownership. *NCTE Beliefs about the Students' Right to Write* states that "[c]ensorship of writing not only stifles student voices but denies students important opportunities to grow as both writers and thinkers," and through authoring visual autobiographies, my "students develop strategies to help them come to understand lessons within the curriculum as well as how their language and ideas can be used to communicate, influence, reflect, explain, analyze, and create" (NCTE, 2014, p. xix).

Students begin by bringing in photos from home, as well as images from magazines, objects, and packaging materials that reveal aspects of their identity and what they most value. They then cut out images in the classroom and share them during our class discussions, developing artifactual literacies—the premise that every object tells a story (Pahl & Rowsell, 2010). I ask questions such as:

- Why did you choose this image?
- Why is it important to you as a person?
- How does it reveal who you are? What story does this image (or the object or person captured by this image) tell?

Images of uncles, cousins, siblings, foods, pets, flags, sports, and words fill the Ziploc baggies that my students keep their collage items in.

I find that students who are usually reluctant to participate in whole-class discussions are vigorously raising their hands, whereas students who often speak while others are speaking find themselves completely engaged by their classmates' stories associated with the images that will make up their collage (Figure 3.1).

One student brought in images of his hometown in Mexico, while another cut out images of dogs. Yet another student brought in a Spanish-language newspaper article that contained a picture of a baseball team. In the picture, he and his mother stood with an award. The students in the class began to comment and ask: "Wow, that's cool! Is that here or in the Dominican Republic?" and "How did you get that award?"

Figure 3.1. A student works on her collage.

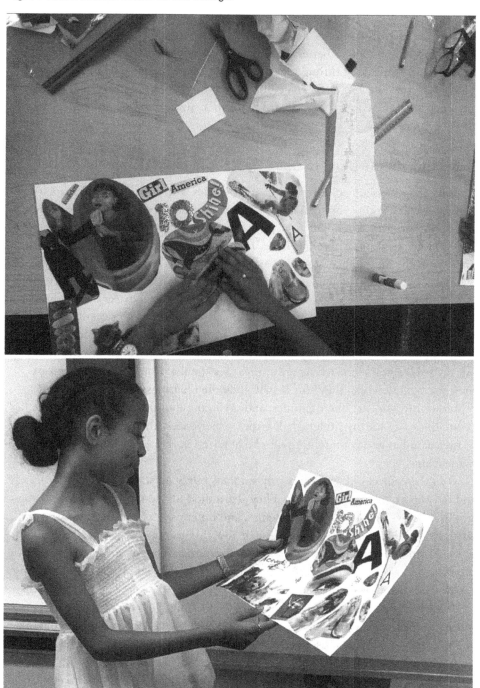

As a teacher, I realized that not only had I been unaware of important aspects of my students' lives that meant so much to them, but also that other students, members of our classroom community, were unaware too. The visual collages allow me to identify students' experiences and funds of knowledge (Moll et al., 1992), thus helping me to better identify and leverage their assets in and through my subsequent teaching throughout the year. Ultimately, this kind of learning lets me sustain their linguistic and cultural practices in my classroom and center my students in my curriculum—their identities, cultural legacies, interests, and language practices.

Reflecting on the Need to Open Up Spaces for Dialogue

Reading these books, exploring students' identities, and creating visual autobiographies—which codify very real issues of power my students experience—open up a space for critical dialogue to happen and for traditional power structures to be troubled and interrupted (Freire, 1970; Souto-Manning, 2010). Although important, the identity work and collages we do and make are done despite the mandated official curriculum adopted by the school. In a way, inspired by Postman and Weingartner (1969), who declared "teaching as a subversive activity" (p. 26), we are participating in subversive curricular actions, which seek to center students' identities and experiences in light of their marginalization and invisiblization in the official curriculum. To be sure, the curriculum guides I have been given throughout my twelve years of teaching are always clear (and at times rigid) in terms of their pacing and scope; they also clearly elide the identities and experiences that represent my students, their families, and their communities. Therefore, I have to create the space for my students' identities, experiences, and practices—and those of their families and communities—to be honored in the classroom, in and through my teaching.

In these spaces of possibility, my students use Spanish and English, separately and in concert, or *translanguaging*. They share their ideas, having "choice and control over topics, forms, language, themes, and other aspects" of their learning and writing (NCTE, 2014, p. xix). I have seen how this empowers all of my students as we affirm one another's backgrounds by listening, asking questions, and learning from and about each other. We revisit these powerful and meaningful learning experiences throughout the year.

When I look back at my twelve years of teaching, I am reassured and recommitted to creating such spaces, where we grow as learners, develop as a community, and strengthen our relationships. As *The Students' Right to Read* reminds us, "One of the most important responsibilities of the English teacher is developing rapport and respect among students. Respect for the uniqueness and potential of the individual . . . should be emphasized" (NCTE, 2018, p. xi). Those relationships are cultivated when students and teachers come together to speak and to comment on what they read, what they hear, and what they fear, coming together and learning as human beings.

In the spaces I have shared in this chapter, students had the opportunity to learn about me and I had the opportunity to learn about them. Together, we developed rapport, but, most important, we came to genuinely care, love, and respect one another—and ourselves. As a result, I found myself committing to opening up, to being vulnerable, as a pedagogical imperative. I no longer regard my vulnerability as a choice, because I recognize the power and possibility of communicating to my students that "no one knows it all; no one is ignorant of everything" (Freire, 1998, p. 39). I realize they have the right to see their experiences and identities reflected in the books they read, as well as in their teachers. They also have the right to explore, understand, and author their own identities. As uncomfortable as it might be, at least at first, it needs to happen.

Recognizing the importance of such tools, spaces, and processes, I am now pushing through my own discomfort and committing to developing and growing such spaces. I find that as I prioritize the development of my students, honor their lives, and value their experiences, I am able to better address learning standards in meaningful ways while also sustaining my students' languages, cultures, and identities. I hope you will join me!

Notes

1. *Ríe, llora . . . a cada cual le llega su hora* can be translated as "laugh, cry . . . everyone's time (eventually) arrives."

2. *Latinx* is a gender-inclusive term referring to people with cultural ties to Latin America and of Latin American descent.

3. "Eurocentricity is based on White supremacist notions whose purposes are to protect White privilege and advantage in education, economics, politics, and so forth" (Asante, 1991, pp. 171–72).

References

Asante, M. K. (1991). The Afrocentric idea in education. *Journal of Negro Education, 60*(2), 170–80.

Bishop, R. S. (1990). Mirrors, windows, and sliding glass doors. *Perspectives, 6*(3), ix–xi. Retrieved from https://scenicregional.org/wp-content/uploads/2017/08/Mirrors-Windows-and-Sliding-Glass-Doors.pdf

Freire, P. (1970). *Pedagogy of the oppressed.* New York, NY: Continuum.

Freire, P. (1998). *Teachers as cultural workers: Letters to those who dare teach.* Boulder, CO: Westview Press.

Ladson-Billings, G. (1995). But that's just good teaching! The case for culturally relevant pedagogy. *Theory Into Practice, 34*(3), 159–65.

Moll, L. C., Amanti, C., Neff, D., & Gonzalez, N. (1992). Funds of knowledge for teaching: Using a qualitative approach to connect homes and classrooms. *Theory Into Practice, 31*(2), 132–41.

National Council of Teachers of English. (2014). *NCTE beliefs about the students' right to write*. Retrieved from http://www2.ncte.org/statement/students-right-to-write/

National Council of Teachers of English. (2018). *The students' right to read*. Retrieved from http://www2.ncte.org/statement/righttoreadguideline/

Pahl, K., & Rowsell, J. (2010). *Artifactual literacies: Every object tells a story*. New York, NY: Teachers College Press.

Postman, N., & Weingartner, C. (1969). *Teaching as a subversive activity*. New York, NY: Delta Book.

Souto-Manning, M. (2010). *Freire, teaching, and learning: Culture circles across contexts*. New York, NY: Peter Lang.

Children's Books

Ada, A. F. (1993). *Me llamo María Isabel* (K. Dyble Thompson, Illus.). New York, NY: Atheneum Books for Young Readers.

Ada, A. F. (2011). *Nacer bailando* (G. M. Zubizarreta, Illus.). New York, NY: Atheneum Books for Young Readers.

Chapter Four

"Learning is mostly about English": Students' Right to Trouble the Language of Power

Emma Pelosi
PS 414K—Brooklyn Arbor School
Brooklyn, NY
and
Patricia (Patty) Pión
PS 503K—School of Discovery
Brooklyn, NY

You don't have to know a bunch of different languages if you don't want to." Patty's second-grade dual language class was seated on the floor, engaged in a discussion as part of that day's social studies lesson. Adriana, a bilingual child fluent in both English and Spanish, had every student's attention with her claim. "So, like, if you don't want to learn other languages, that's fine, 'cause, like, not everyone wants to know the language that someone else speaks." Her comment struck a chord with the class, and a number of hands flew up into the air, accompanied by squeals and eager requests to be the next speaker. Emma, who was student teaching in Patty's class, called on Angelina, an English-dominant student, to respond first.

"I agree and disagree. . . . I disagree with Adriana's thing because I think it's good to know more than one language so then you could actually teach other people more than one, . . . but I do agree with Adriana about how if you don't know one language, maybe you can try to learn it but not actually speak it, but try to learn."

"Well, I have a question then," Emma interjected, using her role as facilitator to direct the students' focus. "Let's open this up to the class. What's the difference between learning and speaking?" She called on Andi, a typically quiet child, to offer her opinion on Angelina's statement. Andi spoke slowly, choosing her words carefully as she organized her thoughts.

"I think that they're different because learning is mostly about English. And speaking different languages . . . you can speak any language that you want." Andi looked around at the class, confident in her opinion, as even more students raised their hands to reply.

This opening scenario illustrates students' perceptions of language hierarchies within the context of a second-grade dual language class, "also known as 'two-way immersion'" (Flores, 2016, p. 30), in a New York City public school. In this particular group, thirteen students had been classified as English-dominant, seven had been classified as Spanish-dominant, and four had been identified as English-Spanish bilingual (not showing a clear preference for either language in their communication). In such a setting, bilingualism is developed within a context that dedicates equal time to instruction in English and in Spanish. Nevertheless, it was clear that students understood how in reality English had primacy in terms of learning. This was reinforced by (a) standardized tests that were English-language only, and (b) the society where they belonged, which deemed English to be superior to Spanish. As Cummins (1994) explained, "The curriculum in schools and the interactions between educators and students reflect the societal power structure in virtually all societies" (p. 153).

Dual language is "an additive form . . . of bilingual education" (Flores, 2016, p. 28), "which place[s] language-majoritized and language-minoritized students together to develop bilingualism in the idealized hegemonic White language practices of English and the home languages of the language-minoritized students" (p. 30). Despite strong support for dual language programs, more than twenty years ago Valdés (1997) issued "a cautionary note" (p. 391). She explained how "[f]or minority children, the acquisition of English is expected. For mainstream children, the acquisition of a non-English language is enthusiastically applauded. Children are aware of these differences" (p. 417).

As explained by Valdés (1997), the focus is "on how well a mainstream child speaks Spanish while ignoring how well a Spanish-speaking child is learning English[, which] sends a very powerful message" about language and power (p. 417). It is within this context, as well as against the background of the National Council of

Teachers of English statements *NCTE Beliefs about Students' Right to Write* (2014) and *The Students' Right to Read* (2018), that we explore issues of language choice in Patty's second-grade dual language classroom as they pertain to students' rights to read, write, and learn.

Language and Power in a Second-Grade Classroom

The students in Patty's class were entering their third year in a dual language (Spanish-English) program. Patty was the classroom teacher, and since she had previously been a kindergarten teacher for the program, she had either taught or known most of the students. Emma was Patty's student teacher that year. We—Patty and Emma—established that our roles would be equal; Emma would be a coteacher, and Patty and Emma would both serve as facilitators and collaborators.

Aiming to foster a learning setting marked by choice and democratic processes, we knew that we would need a strategy for establishing a set of norms to create a space where students could take risks and where their opinions could be shared, a space where discussions would be openly critical and where disagreements grounded on differing perspectives and points of view would be encouraged. Adriana's comment—"if you don't want to learn other languages, that's fine, 'cause . . . not everyone wants to know the language that someone else speaks"—was one of those opportunities. Her comment hovered over the class like a cloud. But the language power dynamic had been established long before her comment was made. Our students' behaviors and reactions gave insight into who felt entitled to participate in classroom conversations and who chose to (or was expected to) opt out and/or silence themselves.

As educators, given our students' verbal and nonverbal reactions, we had to make a decision: We could allow Adriana's comment to fade from the conversation but linger in students' minds, or allow it to be explored in the open and take the class on a magic carpet ride. Better yet, we had the opportunity to allow the students to take *themselves* on this journey. This is what we ultimately chose to do.

"I don't speak Spanish": Troubling Language Hierarchies in a Dual Language Class

The dual language program in which Patty taught was on a 50-50 self-contained roller coaster model, with language division by day. In this model, the language of the day alternated between English and Spanish, with five days of teaching and learning in English and five days of teaching and learning in Spanish in a typical two-week cycle. The idea at the root of this well-known model of bilingual education is that students need to spend equal time engaged in academic learning in each of the languages. To be part of this dual language class, each student's family had made a choice to opt into this bilingual setting with the goal of biliteracy for all the students.

Having spent time with the students on English days (Emma had been assigned to be in Patty's class two days a week), Emma had already begun to form opinions about the various personalities and abilities of the students in the class. However, a couple of weeks into the school year, Emma arrived on a day that was an unexpected Spanish instructional day. Despite not speaking Spanish, Emma decided to stay and observe. That day she learned something that surprised her. Many of the Spanish-dominant students, whom Emma had previously perceived as quieter in class, spoke freely and proudly when their own language was represented as "the language of the day." We agreed that this noticing was worth pursuing, and after a few days of focused observation, Emma noticed a trend. On English days, English-dominant children volunteered to respond more often than their Spanish-dominant classmates did. However, on Spanish days, even though the Spanish-dominant children volunteered more than on English days, the English-dominant children were just as willing to answer, even if their answers were in English.

In one eye-opening moment on a Spanish instructional day, the students had heard a story in Spanish and were asked to write a short response to the story. They were allowed to write in English if they were truly struggling with the task of writing in Spanish. After all, while we wanted "to frame and assign student writing tasks," we agreed that "students should, as much as possible, have choice and control over topics, forms, language, themes, and other aspects of their own writing" (NCTE, 2014, p. xix), including the language employed.

Notwithstanding, Patty had supplemented the story's text with lots of hand gestures and outright translations of the Spanish, and as someone who had never spoken Spanish a day in her life, Emma had no problem following the story. However, most of the English-dominant students completely shut down and refused to write, claiming that they "don't speak Spanish" and "can't do it." When we reminded them that they could write in English, most of them couldn't get past the fact that Spanish was involved and simply repeated their reasoning for giving up.

Reflecting and Preparing for Action

We knew that our next steps, whatever they might be, would need to be chosen carefully. We wanted students to talk about language as both a mode of communication and an aspect of political power, and we wanted to help them develop the tools to critically examine language use (*languaging*) in their own lives. Most important, we wanted our students to leave equipped with the discussion tools and analytic skills to address questions of fairness in their neighborhoods, communities, and social circles. The weeks that followed were full of open-ended questions and student-led inquiries that drove class discussions. We not only sought to foster student choice, but also committed to cultivating the development of their agency and voice.

Our very first lesson was spent discussing the nature of the topics we would explore in the coming weeks. We began with an explanation that the topics we would explore—which included slavery, immigration, discrimination, and nationalism—were so complex that many adults spend their entire lives trying to fully understand them. We also told our students that some of the topics might be very personal and emotional, and that no one, including us, the teachers, would be in a position to judge what others experienced, thought, or believed. All perspectives and points of view would be respected as long as they did not deny the humanity of individuals and/or communities.

Our students, ever rising to meet our high expectations, took their responsibility as empathetic members of a community seriously. They understood that empathy, humanity, and humility, as central pillars of dialogical theory (Freire, 2000), allowed them to grow and learn together instead of simply defending their standpoints in discussions—which, although seemingly dialogical, merely served as side-by-side monologues (Souto-Manning, 2010).

Seeking to access some of the assumptions and beliefs students brought with them, we asked students to answer the following questions:

- Do you think knowing more than one language is important?
- How do you think knowing more than one language could help you?
- What languages do you think we should speak in school? Why?

We used the students' responses to guide our planning of the unit of study.

By the end of the first lesson, our second-grade class had developed a set of community agreements, what they called "rules for discussion," that would be referenced throughout the unit and the rest of the school year (see Figure 4.1):

1. Listen quietly when others are talking.
2. Don't make faces or noises if you don't agree.
3. Don't interrupt.
4. Give people time to think!
5. Be nice!
6. Choose your words carefully.
7. Don't talk under your breath.
8. Let people finish.
9. Don't talk back.
10. Be aware that these topics are sensitive! Be respectful!

Figure 4.1. Rules for discussion.

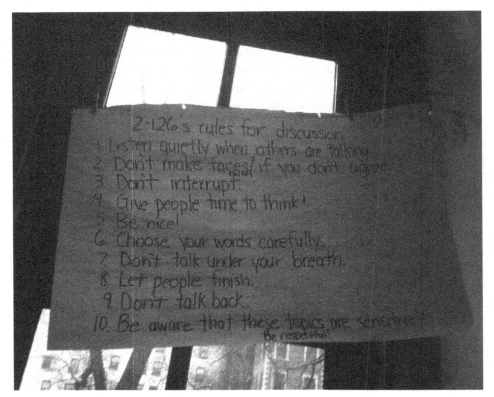

The Unit: A Student-Driven Learning Experience in Dismantling the Linguistic Hierarchy

We began by exploring the history of immigration in the United States, using children's literature as our entry point. Our first picture book, *Coming to America: The Story of Immigration* (Maestro, 1996), took us three full days to complete, despite the fact that we had only planned for one day. The students' critical questions, observations, and discussions were so rich that we had to put our own plans aside to allow them to explore the information through dialoguing, writing, and drawing. On a few occasions, the students felt so compelled to write and discuss their thinking in small groups that we paused our plans to allow them to collectively synthesize writing prompts and questions, respecting their desire to collaborate and write as authentic and intentional acts (Genishi & Dyson, 2009).

We discussed the differences between early immigration and modern-day immigration, and we discussed and problematized the premise of America as a country of immigrants. We transitioned to a study of the linguistic and cultural history of New York City, beginning with when the Dutch "acquired" (yes, we troubled this too!) Manhattan from the Lenape. We discussed the implications of who wrote the official historical accounts of New York City in order to understand colonization processes. Together, we considered how history might have been different if instead of taking the Lenape land, the Dutch had made efforts to learn from, support, and understand the Lenape's ways of being and communicating. This led to an understanding of the multilingual, multiracial, and multicultural makeup of New York City today within a context rife with hierarchies and contradictions—racial, cultural, socioeconomic, and linguistic.

As the class continued to read and learn about the US history of immigration, they became fascinated by Manhattan's transfer of ownership from the Dutch to the English. Although on the surface this particular piece of history seemed unrelated to our students' lives, they connected deeply with this story. This piece of information led to a rich debate about whether the English takeover of Manhattan was fair; after all, some pointed out, the Dutch colonists were experiencing something that reminded them of what they had done to the Lenape who had long inhabited that land. As one child noted, "The Dutch kicked the other people out of their homes and then they come and . . . since they kicked the others . . . out of their homes and they, then they get kicked out."

The importance of language in Manhattan's history did not go unnoticed by the students, either. When one child wondered out loud why the various groups couldn't coexist peacefully on the land, another answered, "Because the other ones wanted to name it the one thing and the other ones wanted to name it the other thing." Although the students had at first thought that Native communities and the Dutch could communicate and perhaps got along, they developed the sophisticated understanding that the Dutch were settler-colonizers who sought to gain "access to Indian labor, land, and resources" (Grande, 2015, p. 23). As a student said, "They [first the Dutch and then the English] wanted to be the owners of the land." Students asked questions and inquired into settler-colonialism, developing a deeper understanding of "systems of colonization . . . fueled by global capitalism" (Grande, 2015, p. 23).

As the unit progressed, we interviewed our students' families to develop a richer understanding of our own locations and collective histories. Several family members agreed to be interviewed about their own experiences and histories. In small groups, the students eagerly asked family members questions that they had developed. This helped them to understand bilingualism and multilingualism as norms in many families across time and space. In asking families about language

loss ("My grandpa used to speak Spanish"), the children learned about the construction of English—dominant American English in particular—as the language
of power. They came to see that it was not a superior language, but it had been
constructed over time as dominant because it was the language of those who had
power (Delpit, 1988).

Much of our time was spent critically reading books and other texts. Concur-
rently, the children collectively engaged in problematizing the world and society
of which we were part in terms of language and power (Freire, 1985). As teachers,
we were guided by *The Students' Right to Read*, which states, "Freedom of inquiry
is essential to education in a democracy" (NCTE, 2018, p. xvii). Through explorations of immigration, slavery, discrimination, and patriotism, we worked with
students to develop their understanding of language and the multifaceted role it
plays in how we interact as members of a society. We were amazed by the insight
that each student brought to the discussions, and each lesson concluded with the
same question, driven by the class: How did our views of language and communication change when we considered perspectives beyond our own? In one discussion, a student commented: "Well, when you speak your own language, you're like,
'What are they saying?' It doesn't really sound like they're saying a word. But . . .
you realize that they're speaking their own language . . . and they're thinking about
you: 'What are *you* saying?'" As she elaborated on her revelation, she shared with
the class an understanding that other languages may sound different from her own,
but that they serve the same function of communicating and making connections
with others.

Near the end of the semester, the conversations turned to how the class could
transform their new perspectives into actions that could be implemented in the
classroom and in the greater world. We opened the lesson with a simple question:
"Why do you think we (Patty and Emma) chose to study language practices in
such depth?" We asked this question because we wanted to "avoid indoctrination
because of personal beliefs" (NCTE, 2014, p. xix). As this unit's relevance in the
classroom became even clearer to the children, they worked together to brainstorm
ways that they could value English and Spanish equally, interrupting traditional
language hierarchies. Their ideas exemplified the empathy and sense of civic responsibility that the class had come to own; their suggestions included encouraging
the government to "divide [language use in government] fairly between English
and Spanish," breaking up into smaller study groups daily to practice speaking a
new language, increasing the use of Spanish "by 2% each day" until English and
Spanish felt equally valued, and forging friendships with people who speak other
languages.

Looking Back, Moving Forward

As we reflected on this learning journey, we considered: Did all the students eventually change their opinions about language? Some did and some didn't. What did change were the classroom conversations. Instead of privileging English uncritically, students constantly troubled the use of English in the classroom, especially on Spanish instructional days or when responding to books read in Spanish. This second-grade class became a group of conversationalists who used inquiry and dialogue to enhance their learning. They used their words and their languages to further educate themselves—and their teachers.

One child, Andi—who earlier in the year had drawn the distinction between learning and speaking—expressed that she thought both English and Spanish were important because we speak *both* of them at school. It seemed that learning was no longer "mostly about English," as she had previously believed. She had developed an understanding that she could learn in a classroom where both languages were welcome and present every day. All in all, the second graders came to understand that languages and "[w]ords are . . . powerful tool[s] of expression, a means to clarify, explore, inquire, and learn as well as a way to record present moments for the benefit of future generations" (NCTE, 2014, p. xix), in both written and oral forms.

References

Cummins, J. (1994). Lies we live by: National identity and social justice. *International Journal of the Sociology of Language, 110*, 145–54.

Delpit, L. D. (1988). The silenced dialogue: Power and pedagogy in educating other people's children. *Harvard Educational Review, 58*(3), 280–98.

Flores, N. (2016). A tale of two visions: Hegemonic whiteness and bilingual education. *Educational Policy, 30*(1), 13–38.

Freire, P. (1985). Reading the world and reading the word: An interview with Paulo Freire. *Language Arts, 62*(1), 15–21.

Freire, P. (2000). *Pedagogy of the oppressed* (30th anniversary ed.). New York, NY: Continuum.

Genishi, C., & Dyson, A. H. (2009). *Children, language, and literacy: Diverse learners in diverse times.* New York, NY: Teachers College Press.

Grande, S. (2015). *Red pedagogy: Native American social and political thought* (10th anniversary ed.). Lanham, MD: Rowman & Littlefield.

National Council of Teachers of English. (2014). *NCTE beliefs about the students' right to write.* Retrieved from http://www2.ncte.org/statement/students-right-to-write/

National Council of Teachers of English. (2018). *The students' right to read.* Retrieved from http://www2.ncte.org/statement/righttoreadguideline/

Souto-Manning, M. (2010). *Freire, teaching, and learning: Culture circles across contexts.* New York, NY: Peter Lang.

Valdés, G. (1997). Dual-language immersion programs: A cautionary note concerning the education of language-minority students. *Harvard Educational Review, 67*(3), 391–425.

Children's Book

Maestro, B. (1996). *Coming to America: The story of immigration* (S. Ryan, Illus.). New York, NY: Scholastic.

Chapter Five

Students' Rights to Read and Write about Homophobia and Hate Crimes

Jessica Martell and William "Billy" Fong
Central Park East II
New York, NY

> "An Act of Terror, an Act of Hate: 50 Killed in Orlando Gay Nightclub"
> (Headline from *Los Angeles Times*)
>
> "Praising ISIS, Gunman Attacks Gay Nightclub, Leaving 50 Dead in Worst Shooting on US Soil"
> (Headline from *The New York Times*)
>
> "A Night of Terror in Orlando"
> (Headline from *The Wall Street Journal*)
>
> "50 Killed at Gay Club in Fla."
> (Headline from *The Washington Post*)
>
> "Massacre: Orlando Mass Shooting Deadliest in US History"
> (Headline from *USA Today*)

These were the newspaper headlines that we—Jessica and Billy—woke up to on Sunday morning of June 12, 2016, along with gripping footage of distraught patrons experiencing shock, fear, and a wide array of emotions at the scene of the shooting, which took place at the Pulse nightclub in Orlando, Florida. Fifty people were killed and fifty-eight were wounded in a terrorist attack and hate crime inside Pulse at 2:00 a.m. that day. Pulse is a gay nightclub with many patrons who are part of the LGBTQ+ community or are allies. Omar Mateen, a 29-year-old from Port St. Lucie, Florida, was the shooter; he had made 911 calls earlier that day to communicate his allegiance to ISIS. At the time, it was the deadliest mass shooting in US history. It was all over the news. We knew our students had learned about it, just as we had. We also knew that it was our responsibility to address this event in our fourth-grade classroom the next day.

We were keenly aware that some students would come to school with opinions, doubts, questions, and wonderings on Monday, the day after the shootings. Unfortunately, Jessica, a cisgender straight female, had previously planned to be out on that Monday. We talked and realized that both of us were experiencing anxiety at the thought of Billy, a cisgender gay male, addressing this topic with the students by himself, without an ally in the room. We worried that the larger community might see our addressing this as Billy pushing a "gay agenda."

Although we knew that it was everyone's responsibility to interrupt injustice and foster justice of any kind in and through teaching, we experienced a contradiction: we were reluctant for Billy, a gay man, to address the homophobic hate crime, the act of terrorism, that had taken place. Had Jessica been there, this would not have been an issue. Nevertheless, we knew we had to address the Pulse shootings despite these concerns and despite our previous plans. It was our responsibility; it was also our students' right.

Pulse and/in Our Teaching?

For the entirety of the school year, we were committed to creating a space in our shared classroom where students could engage in brave dialogues that troubled and sought to interrupt racism, social inequities, sexism, and homophobia, among many topics pertaining to societal injustices and related bigotries. We had engaged our students in the process captured by the "critical cycle" (see Figure 5.1), in which they read their worlds, identified injustices (such as the marginalization or invisiblization of certain people's histories), problematized them, engaged in dialogue, and collectively problem-solved, seeking to take action and promote transformation (Souto-Manning, 2010). Often the injustices identified were codified and represented by a storybook, picture, or video. This allowed us to position the issues students brought up within a variety of contexts collectively—not as the isolated problem of any one student.

Although we had a process in place for working through issues of injustice, we both wondered whether we should wait until Tuesday, when Jessica would be back in class, to discuss how the children had experienced the Pulse events and how they were feeling. This would mean that students would have to wait for the time

Figure 5.1. The critical cycle (inspired by Souto-Manning, 2010).

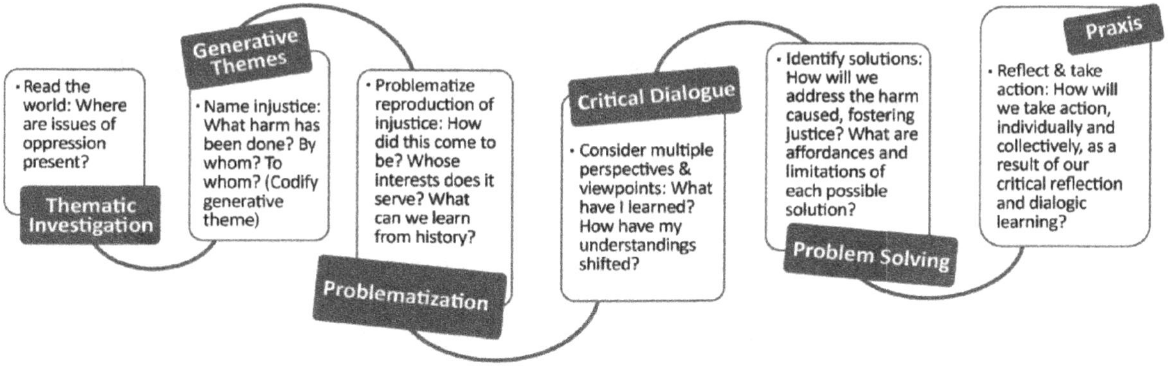

Thematic Investigation
- Read the world: Where are issues of oppression present?

Generative Themes
- Name injustice: What harm has been done? By whom? To whom? (Codify generative theme)

Problematization
- Problematize reproduction of injustice: How did this come to be? Whose interests does it serve? What can we learn from history?

Critical Dialogue
- Consider multiple perspectives & viewpoints: What have I learned? How have my understandings shifted?

Problem Solving
- Identify solutions: How will we address the harm caused, fostering justice? What are affordances and limitations of each possible solution?

Praxis
- Reflect & take action: How will we take action, individually and collectively, as a result of our critical reflection and dialogic learning?

and space to express themselves. Ultimately, we decided to proceed with Billy facilitating the discussion by himself on Monday. Despite her initial reluctance, Jessica realized that no one should have to wait for the cisgender straight teacher to facilitate a conversation that would eventually address discrimination and hate crimes, and that she was not the most important member in the community. That is, she came to the realization that this critical learning moment could take place without her. Additionally, in talking with Jessica, Billy eventually realized that although he was especially emotionally affected by this event due to his deep ties with the LGBTQ+ community, the Pulse nightclub incident transcended LGBTQ+ issues; it was an act of terrorism against humanity. If he made this lesson about him, then he would in fact be promoting a "gay agenda."

With our anxieties set aside, we started considering what materials we would utilize to ensure a productive dialogue would occur. We wanted to find materials that allowed students to grapple with the issues and express their ideas and feelings. Serendipitously, June 12, 2016, was the night of the Tony Awards. Upon accepting the award for best original score for *Hamilton*, Lin-Manuel Miranda delivered a heartfelt speech that addressed the mass killings at Pulse, which had taken place earlier that day (excerpted here):

> We live through times when hate and fear seem stronger
> We rise and fall and light from dying embers
> Remembrances that hope and love lasts long
> And love is love is love is love is love is love is love is love is love. . . .
>
> (Miranda, 2016)

Using Miranda's speech as a core text and framing questions that would be posed to students carefully, Billy and Jessica were ready for whatever would come on Monday morning.

Students' Rights to Read and Write about Homophobia and Hate Crimes

We teach at Central Park East II (CPE2), a progressive public elementary school in East Harlem, New York City. Social justice is one of our school's core values. The students at CPE2 are a racially, socioeconomically, and academically diverse group of learners. This was not the first time our fourth graders had heard of a mass shooting. It was also not the first time they had heard of someone getting killed through the use of a gun. However, it was the first time many of them came to school on Monday talking about the shootings and referring to the tragedy as a "hate crime."

We knew many of the students had heard of the hit Broadway musical *Hamilton* and were fans of its writer and producer, Lin-Manuel Miranda (a New Yorker, like them); some of the students had even seen the musical. So we decided to play Miranda's acceptance speech for the students. Additionally, we located a Newsela article titled "Shooting at Florida Club Kills 50, Called an 'Act of Terrorism'" to help facilitate discussion, in case any students were unaware of this current event. We accessed Newsela because it's a database of current events stories especially for classroom use. We knew it was important to protect students' right to read about potentially controversial topics, and we selected our texts in order to foster "the investigation of ideas . . . rather [than] the indoctrination of a certain set of beliefs" (National Council of Teachers of English, 2018, p. vii).

Upholding Students' Right to Explore Controversial Topics

Unsure what students knew, Billy started the discussion during the social studies block that Monday by asking the students if they had heard of anything that happened over the weekend. Some fourth graders started thinking individually, while some started whispering the same question to each other in hopes of jogging their own memories. While students were whispering and the volume of the discussions increased, Billy nudged, ". . . something that happened in Florida?"

At that moment, eyes widened and hands immediately shot up. Many students recalled relevant and accurate details. The only inaccurate detail was the number of deaths, ranging from small numbers to ridiculously large ones. A couple of students said, "A lot of people were killed in Florida," or, "There was a guy that shot lots of people and I want to say that some people think that guy is a terrorist."

As some students shared, others interjected with the following thoughts: "Yeah, but it was mainly gay people that were killed," or, "Yeah! And Lin-Manuel Miranda even spoke about this last night!" *Hamilton* was popular during this time, and Jessica and Billy had spoken about the ethnic and cultural origins of its writer, Lin-Manuel Miranda, as part of our efforts to resolve the injustices in representations of people of color and their achievements in popular culture.

Many students shared what they recalled. After a number of shares, Billy asked, "Any more recollections or new information?" Upon encountering silence, Billy directed students to the Newsela article recapping the incident and did a shared reading with the students to process the information. He recognized that some students were hearing this information for the first time. They needed time to process the events and get more information from an informational text source.

After the students read "Shooting at Florida Club Kills 50, Called an 'Act of Terrorism'," Billy showed them the first question he wanted them to respond to on a sticky note. The question addressed their feelings about Omar Mateen's attack at Pulse. When students were done, they placed their responses on the anchor chart[1] (Figure 5.2). These are a few of the responses students wrote (although we have altered the spelling of words for readability, we did not make other edits or revisions, because we sought to honor the voices of our students):

- How I feel about Omar Mateen's attack is shock because nobody knows why he did it. Was it on purpose?
- I feel that this is about gay rights because it happened in a gay nightclub.
- Depressed, because all these people got killed for no particular reason and it should not have happened at all.
- I feel worried about going to Florida because I wonder if there will be more.
- I feel angry about the attack because I hate gun violence and especially massacres. I want to give mercy to the lost ones.
- I feel horrible because people should be able to go to a nightclub, be out instead of being scared and shot.
- I feel very upset. I believe everyone has rights so no one can judge you. After all, you can't judge a book by its cover.

After some students shared their responses orally, Billy directed them to Lin-Manuel Miranda's speech and showed them the second question they would be responding to: "How does Lin-Manuel Miranda's speech speak to the attack?" The students listened to the speech, received a hard copy of the speech, and again wrote their responses on sticky notes. These are some of their responses:

- I think it [Miranda's speech] relates to it [the attack at Pulse] because it shows that we should never lose hope.

- I think it has to do with what happened in Florida because it says we live through times when hate and fear seem stronger. And he repeats love is love.
- I think it was nice of him to write this speech because he was speaking out about the attacks.
- He said love is love is love because love is strong. The poem is about how love can never be broken even through the hardest times.

Billy and the students concluded the first day's exploration by discussing students' thoughts in response to the second question.

When Jessica rejoined the class on Tuesday, we had another anchor chart with two questions. As a whole class, we tackled the first question, which was:

Figure 5.2. Students' first questions about the Pulse nightclub shooting.

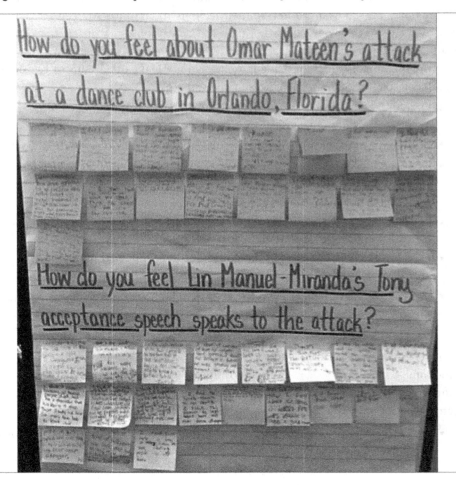

"What is REALLY the problem with the Pulse shooting?" Students again offered their ideas on sticky notes. Together we compared responses and created larger categories. Many students immediately said "gay rights," "gun control," and "gun violence." These we wrote on the anchor chart (see Figure 5.3).

One student proposed Muslims as a problem and raised relevant questions, which informed our dialogue about the religion of Islam. Although initially misguided, this student's questions identified common myths about Islam, such as equating Islam with terrorism and Muslims with terrorists. After posing questions such as "Where did you hear this?" and "Do you have a personal experience that justifies or supports your point of view?," we asked the class if anyone practiced Islam or knew of people who did. Many students affirmatively responded that they knew someone who was Muslim. We asked them to describe the Muslim people they knew. Their descriptions focused on generosity, kindness, and selflessness;

Figure 5.3. Second anchor chart.

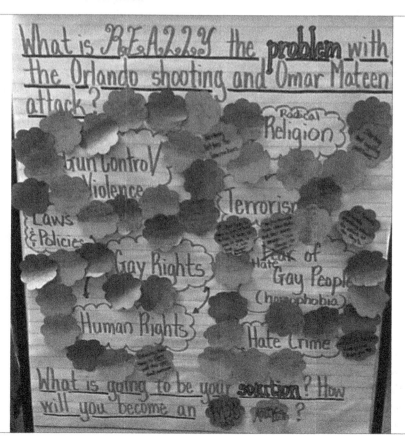

they did not reflect any inkling of terrorism or hate. We then asked whether practicing Islam as a religion was the problem. Students, empathizing with Muslim individuals they knew, concluded that *radicalizing* Islam was the issue. They also agreed that the media should not equate Muslims and terrorists or Islam and radicalism. As one of them said, "That's just wrong!"

Typical of teachers, we shared with students that it is important to consider the source of problems in our society, to question what we hear, and to dismantle stereotypes, but we emphasized that it is also essential to think of solutions and be everyday activists. We showed students Lin-Manuel Miranda's speech (2016) again and shared our view that his choice to speak at the Tony Awards about this incident was a form of activism and at least a partial solution to the problem. We asked them: "What is going to be your solution? How will you become an EVERYDAY ACTIVIST?"

We asked students to return to their independent tables with sticky notes to write down two solutions that addressed problems identified by the texts they had discussed: the Newsela article and the video of Lin-Manual Miranda's speech. In response to the question about what actions they might take, responses included:

- Not dislike gay people. I can tell people what is wrong and what is right.
- Not dislike gay people and become friends with gay people.
- Stand up with gay people.
- All gay people should have rights.
- Let people be who they want to be.
- Change the gun laws in society.
- Have more gun laws.
- Tell people to stop using guns.
- Participating in community protests against terrorism.
- More research on this so I could find more solutions.

Students had a variety of their own problems they could have addressed, but many focused on resolving the problem of gay rights (or homophobia), terrorism (or acceptance), and/or gun laws/violence.

Through the use of Souto-Manning's critical cycle (2010), our students read, listened, analyzed (via dialogue, sticky notes, and charts), discussed relevant systematic and critical issues, problematized (through their potential solutions), and took action against this social injustice. As they problematized the Pulse shooting, students were able to identify homophobia and hate as foundational to the hate crime that had taken place on Sunday, June 12, 2016. They talked about issues of fairness and inclusion. They talked about the humanity of LGBTQ+ individuals and communities as a matter of justice. They were convinced that they wanted to advocate for LGBTQ+ rights, to "stand with gay people." It was a matter of love, as they had heard in Miranda's speech. Then they problem-solved and moved on to plot and engage in action.

Students took further action by creating a fundraiser that generated more than $300. In determining where the proceeds would be donated, students chose between three organizations that we teachers narrowed down: the Ben Cohen Foundation, It Gets Better, and the Trevor Project. The students ultimately selected the Trevor Project, a national organization that provides crisis intervention and suicide prevention for LGBTQ+ youth. Because we had the privilege of looping with our students, remaining with the same group for two school years, this last activity happened during National Friendship Month in February of the following school year. Nevertheless, when debating between which antibullying organization the proceeds should go to, many students referenced the Pulse incident and Lin-Manuel Miranda's speech to support their choice. Thus, in providing students a space to discuss this controversial event, they were able not only to read injustices in their world, but also to take steps to trouble them and rewrite more just tomorrows. They were developing not only as capable readers and writers, but also as lasting, powerful activists.

Implications for Teachers Seeking to Address Similar Topics

As our students engaged in meaningful dialogue around the issues that affect LGBTQ+ communities, we were able to help develop their literacies through the use of resources such as Newsela, other news articles, and speeches, thus linking issues of justice and human rights to high expectations for academic literacy development (Ladson-Billings, 1995). Using these resources, our students were able to gather information on the impact of the Pulse nightclub shooting, including unpacking homophobic biases and acts of crime against LGBTQ+ communities throughout their city, state, and country. They read informational texts, compared perspectives, and synthesized arguments. They wrote informational texts. They wrote letters. They developed as readers and writers. Further, they grew as active citizens committed to fostering LGBTQ justice.

We thus encourage teachers seeking to address homophobia and hate crimes in and through their teaching not to position such commitments in opposition to academic pressures and demands. We hope that our chapter shows how academically rigorous and socially just teaching can and should go hand in hand.

Note

1. We use anchor charts (poster size paper, on an easel) to record important ideas and strategies, honoring our students' experiences and ideas while "anchoring" their learning.

References

Ladson-Billings, G. (1995). But that's just good teaching! The case for culturally relevant pedagogy. *Theory Into Practice, 34*(3), 159–65.

Miranda, L-M. (2016). *Acceptance speech, best score: Lin-Manuel Miranda* [Tony Awards]. Retrieved from https://www.youtube.com/watch?v=6jehrbUGdlE

National Council of Teachers of English. (2018). *The students' right to read.* Retrieved from http://www2.ncte.org/statement/righttoreadguideline/

Souto-Manning, M. (2010). *Freire, teaching, and learning: Culture circles across contexts.* New York, NY: Peter Lang.

Students' Right to Trauma-Informed Literacy Teaching

Chapter Six

Karina Malik
M103–Dos Puentes Elementary School
New York, NY

As I prepared for a new class of first graders, I thought about my plan for the day. I kept asking myself the same questions: Have I taken into account the various identities, experiences, and needs of my soon-to-be students? How will I help my classroom community cultivate and sustain a culture of care and understanding?

Soon it was time to welcome families and students into the classroom. As children walked in, they each received their name tag and were guided to their seat. Each table had a box of manipulatives for students to interact with while everyone settled in. Suddenly the shriek and cry of a student directed my attention toward one table. "It was Josiah!" another student yelled and pointed. In response, Josiah (a pseudonym) quickly hid under the table.

This was not the first time I had heard the name Josiah. I had heard about him the year before, in meetings, in the office, from other teachers and students. I had even been warned about him. I knew I would be his teacher, and I spent a large portion of the summer thinking about how I would support his development in my classroom. Josiah is a student labeled with emotional disturbance who already had a reputation among his classmates and adults even before walking into my classroom. I thought I could prepare for a student like Josiah by reading as many articles about emotional disturbance as I could get my hands on. But I was wrong. I and many teachers are confronted "with a serious dilemma: how to balance their primary mission of education with the reality that many students need help in dealing with traumatic stress to attend regularly and engage in the learning process" (Ko et al., 2008, p. 398).

During the first month of school, Josiah's behavior became more disruptive. He hurt other students, yelled, and threatened adults. He disrupted whole-group lessons and neighboring classrooms. I implemented several behavior interventions with little to no results, not understanding how practices "that regulate students' behavior are another way schools may be traumatizing students" (Gaffney, 2019). To be sure, I had not fully accounted for "how schools themselves can induce trauma" (Gaffney, 2019). I had to show Josiah that I loved him and cared for him, even when he struggled to communicate or process his emotions. These understandings—along with the knowledge that "teaching about trauma is not the same as trauma-informed teaching" (Carello & Butler, 2014)—were crucial for my understanding of trauma-informed teaching and for the development of our relationship.

As the National Council of Teachers of English has stated in its position statement *The Students' Right to Read*, teachers "may use different texts for different purposes" (NCTE, 2018, p. x). Here I explain how I used trauma-informed literature as a pathway to inclusion, rather than selecting literature based solely on learning standards or curricular scopes. Students have the right to read books that "keep students in touch with the reality of the world" (p. xi) they are experiencing in and out of the classroom. Throughout this chapter, I highlight how students' right to read entails reading and engaging with literature they can relate to, particularly for students like Josiah who are constantly punished for showing emotion. This is especially pertinent during early childhood, when children are beginning to understand fears, frustrations, joys, and hope. Reading books that depict these emotions in ways that authentically reflect the students' own emotions can serve as a pathway for students to work through their emotions and begin to understand trauma.

Understanding Trauma

Trauma is not something that we hear, talk about, or are prepared to handle as teachers. Yet it is too often part of young children's lives and stories. The likelihood of us teaching a student who has experienced trauma is high, and thus we teachers must be prepared to support the authoring of trauma-focused stories. Too often, issues of trauma are shut down in the classroom due to our lack of comfort or preparation for providing support as students try to make sense of trauma in their lives through writing, talking, or story acting. Despite most teachers' lack of preparation or comfort, a 2017 study found that incorporating social-emotional learning interventions into the classroom has the ability to decrease disruptive behavior and increase academic success long term (Taylor et al., 2017). Family and community violence or being victims of abuse are some of the traumas my students have experienced. As a teacher committed to offering all of my students opportunities to author their own stories, I strive to maintain a trauma-informed classroom.

It can be challenging to address issues of trauma in the classroom. There are so many misconceptions surrounding early childhood trauma, such as the belief that students ages 0–6 are too young to understand or internalize trauma. This falsehood is easily believed because students so young may not clearly verbalize their feelings or recount such events orally or in writing. Although it is true that sometimes students may not fully understand traumatic incidents or events, this does not mean that such situations will not affect them, their learning, and their development. This is why we teachers must have trauma-informed literature available to facilitate conversations that have the potential to lead to better understandings and safer spaces in our classrooms. As Flecha explained, "trauma-informed education is most effectively implemented through . . . school and classroom systems in ways that allow every child to access an equitable education without demanding each child share their stories. None of us are entitled to the details of a child's pain" (Torres, 2018).

Additionally, while we want the best for the children we teach and will do our best to provide a safe and nurturing learning environment, circumstances or systemic reasons can be obstacles preventing this from happening. I have found that first and foremost, it is important to distinguish a systemic issue from an individual issue: "Treating individual traumas without naming systemic injustice . . . means schools don't just risk leaving some traumas unrecognized; it means they risk retraumatizing students" (Gaffney, 2019). Also, it isn't fair or helpful to our students when we enter into a rhetoric of blame, especially when the blame is directed toward the adult who is closest to them. Blaming will not make the trauma go away. While it may make us temporarily feel better, it is ultimately unhelpful to our students.

In this chapter, I discuss how I realized how prevalent the impact of trauma is in the lives of the children I teach and in the lives of children in general throughout the United States (Gaffney, 2019). I share my own journey following this realization, explaining how I worked to become better equipped to create a trauma-informed classroom for my students; a classroom where stigmatized behaviors are commonly troubled and systemic injustices are routinely named. In what follows, I share how we, as a class, begin the year by creating a safe environment of trust and transparency and continue to work together to build a supportive environment that empowers students' voices and stories. I conclude by sharing how I respond to trauma in my classroom. In doing so, I share resources I have identified over the years in hopes that they may prove helpful to other teachers seeking to foster trauma-informed classrooms.

Addressing the Roots and Symptoms of Trauma in My Classroom

Following the episode that opens this chapter, I discovered that Josiah had experienced trauma during his early childhood years. His experience with trauma as a result of systemic injustices affecting his family uniquely affected him as he was still developing an understanding of cause and effect. Through conversations with me and routine exchanges with classmates, Josiah continuously blamed himself and/or his caregivers for the trauma he had experienced. He blamed me and his classmates for not avoiding a particular traumatic event or changing the result of it. This was heartbreaking. During breakdowns and outbursts, while I was being blamed, it was crucial for me as an educator not to fall into the trap of blaming Josiah or his family. Instead, it was essential for me to understand that when trauma happens students can begin to exhibit negative feelings about themselves and those around them. This helped me to not take Josiah's actions and reactions personally, but instead to understand them as a by-product of his experience of trauma. Josiah is not an exception. Students in my classroom have experienced abuse and neglect, exposure to community and domestic violence, refugee trauma, sexual abuse, and medical trauma. While initially shocking and potentially alarming, this is not unusual; according to the Centers for Disease Control and Prevention, one in four children experience some form of child abuse or neglect in their lifetimes (2019).

Within my first-grade inclusive class (comprising twenty-six bilingual children with and without identified disabilities), my students and I work every day to help them identify their own strengths in order to reverse negative self-talk and ideas. I purposefully work with each child I teach to identify their strengths, and I then leverage these strengths in my teaching. Additionally, we work together daily to identify our emotions and work through them.

At the beginning of the year, as a class community we develop an "emotion wall." We determine which emotions we want to include on our wall, such as *happy*, *sad*, *tired*, *confused*, *mad*, and *other* (because not all emotions can be described in just one word). Throughout the course of the school year, we discuss which emotions we want to add to or take away from our wall. As a routine, every morning students walk into the classroom and identify how they feel by placing their picture underneath an emotion. This helps them become aware of their feelings—and also to know each other's feelings. As NCTE reminds us: "One of the most important responsibilities of the . . . teacher is developing rapport and respect among students. Respect for the uniqueness and potential of the individual . . . should be emphasized" (2018, p. xi). This is what I sought to build through the construction of an emotion wall, which provided the opening for talking about our feelings as individuals and as a collective.

To develop our understandings of emotions, as a class we read books like *Knuffle Bunny* (2004) by Mo Willems. We explore how Trixie, the main character, feels when she loses her favorite bunny. Students have the opportunity to talk about their experiences with losing something or about a time when something made them sad. This is especially important because some students experiencing trauma are homeless or transient and tend to lose things—yet are often chastised in school for doing so. Other books that serve as tools for facilitating discussions about feelings include:

- *Anh's Anger* (2009) by Gail Silver
- *Hurty Feelings* (2004) by Helen Lester
- *Sometimes I Feel Awful* (2003) by Joan Singleton Prestine
- *Steps and Stones* (2011) by Gail Silver
- *The Very Lonely Firefly* (1995) by Eric Carle

Alexander and the Terrible, Horrible, No Good, Very Bad Day (1987) by Judith Viorst is a book I often read in my classroom to facilitate discussions around being angry or mad. As I read the book aloud, I engage my students in identifying the ways in which the main character is confronted with multiple situations that make him angry and that he has no control over. We then discuss how Alexander could have dealt with his emotions, while also acknowledging that many of the incidents were outside of his control. Students also share what helps them when they are feeling angry or mad. As a class, we chart out the different strategies we can use when we are feeling upset. Responses range from counting and breathing in and out to sitting in our "peace corner" and rolling therapeutic putty as a coping tool for releasing tension (McConnico, Boynton-Jarrett, Bailey, & Nandi, 2016).

Throughout the year, I strategically choose books to read aloud with students that include characters who embody confidence, positive self-talk, perseverance, and resilience. These are some of the books that address issues important to my students, many of which are at the root of their trauma, such as homelessness, transnational separations, and parental incarceration:

- *A Shelter in Our Car* (2004) by Monica Gunning
- *Dear Primo* (2010) by Duncan Tonatiuh
- *Let's Go See Papá!* (2011) by Lawrence Schimel and Alba Marina Rivera
- *Visiting Day* (2002) by Jacqueline Woodson

Not all students are ready to, or want to, address their own experiences with trauma as we read these books aloud and discuss them. While I don't expect students to share their stories of trauma, my hope is that by reading such books, students will realize that the trauma they have experienced is not their fault. Further, I hope that they will understand that our classroom is a site where trauma is not silenced or marginalized. In my experience, early childhood classrooms seldom confront the topic of trauma holistically. Instead, it's something to be addressed on a case-by-case basis, framed as a problem of individual children. This was the case for Josiah, who was asked to talk about his emotions only when he had an outburst. Talking about his emotions was used as a consequence of his perceived misbehavior, which led to his belief that talking was always a punishment, rather than an opportunity to feel free to explore the emotions that stemmed from his trauma.

In viewing trauma as a collective issue central to teaching and learning, I have found that having books about trauma available can be incredibly empowering for children. Coupled with discussions, these books communicate to children that they are not alone, and that with the support of others, they can begin to work through their past experiences. Additionally, we read books with characters who succeed and/or fail in everyday situations: in their best efforts to learn to whistle, to reach their final destination, to not get distracted and frustrated by noise. These books, while not addressing the roots of trauma, serve as powerful tools for discussing its symptoms as visible in the classroom through everyday interactions.

During the reading of each text, we identify the problem and discuss possible solutions. We critically analyze each solution and address failure as a possible option. We continuously revisit these questions and scenarios in different books throughout the year, including:

- *The Little Engine That Could* (1976) by Watty Piper
- *Too Loud Lily* (2004) by Sofie Laguna
- *Whistle for Willie* (1964) by Ezra Jack Keats

Although I do my best to have materials and read-alouds that address the roots and symptoms of trauma, I don't always have books that meet every child's individual experiences and reactions to those experiences. I have come to learn over the years that because students are so vulnerable at this age, the way each child experiences trauma is unique; therefore, no single book will meet the individual needs of every child. I am also aware that, as Dulce-Marie Flecha underscored:

trauma-informed teaching is not a content, but a method for teaching content. It is at its absolute best when built into our daily routines, classroom space, instructional strategies, and school-wide systems. Reading a book that features a character experiencing trauma means very little if our methodology is inaccessible to students experiencing trauma. (Torres, 2018)

Addressing Issues of Trauma for Young People

Young children exhibit both physiological and behavioral symptoms linked to the trauma they have suffered. The way these symptoms manifest within early childhood are unique to each child because this particular age group is still developing the ability to express feelings. Additionally, at the age of five, six, or seven, my first-grade students are still learning how to keep themselves safe and how to know when they are in dangerous situations. They rely heavily on the guidance of a caregiver or adult for their own well-being. If the caregiver is also affected by trauma, the relationship between the child and the caregiver can easily become challenging and stressful. So, in addition to reading books about the roots and symptoms of trauma, we read books that address an array of family relationships.

In an effort to begin to address family relationships within the classroom without singling students out or making their experience(s) of trauma the topic of our learning, I introduce, read, and discuss a variety of children's books. A popular book that facilitates discussions is *Koala Lou* (1988) by Mem Fox. Koala Lou's caregiver becomes overwhelmed with other daily tasks and forgets to tell Koala Lou how much she loves her. Koala enters an event with the intention of winning, not realizing that unconsciously, she is also competing for her mother's love and attention. As a class, we discuss times when we have tried to get the attention of a caregiver who has been too busy to respond. We identify how common this situation is and, without normalizing it, discuss how it makes us feel. Many students verbalize feeling upset, neglected, or frustrated. After reading and discussing the story in relation to our experiences, making text-to-self and text-to-world connections, as a class we aim to recognize these feelings and that we are not alone, that others sometimes feel the same way. We go on to discuss other behaviors that may arise as a consequence, because when the support of a caregiver is absent, children may feel conflicting emotions and exhibit behaviors that are difficult for educators to understand and address. Some of these behaviors include excessive temper, aggressiveness, verbal abuse, excessive screaming or crying, being easily startled, anxiety, fear, avoidance, and demanding attention through both positive and negative behaviors. Making such reactions visible offers children a new lens for seeing other children who may engage in such behaviors; they come to understand the behavior as an enactment of the child's feelings, as opposed to signaling that the child is "bad." In this way, we start to construct a trauma-informed classroom. While we do not seek to normalize trauma, we do not blame children for their experiences and behaviors related to trauma.

Implications for Teachers and Teaching in Trauma-Informed Ways

While many educators perceive behaviors such as excessive temper, aggressiveness, verbal abuse, excessive screaming or crying, anxiety, avoidance, and ongoing demands for attention as problematic, or blame the child without regard for the reasons behind these behaviors, it is important to understand that these behaviors may result from traumatized children's difficulty self-regulating. Instead of jumping to judgments, which are likely to create oppositional relationships and further conflicts, I encourage early childhood educators to address these behaviors and emotions through literature. Read-alouds can be incredibly powerful resources. In addition to the books identified earlier, over the years I have identified a number of texts that have been helpful tools for discussing family relationships and addressing issues of trauma in my own classroom. Some of these books are:

- *Don't Forget I Love You* (2004) by Mariam Moss
- *Full, Full, Full of Love* (2008) by Trish Cooke
- *Guji Guji* (2004) by Chih-Yuan Chen
- *I Love You the Purplest* (1996) by Barbara M. Joose
- *Ladder to the Moon* (2011) by Maya Soetoro-Ng
- *Max and the Tag-Along Moon* (2013) by Floyd Cooper
- *Niño Wrestles the World* (2013) by Yuyi Morales
- *Soup Day* (2010) by Melissa Iwai
- *The Kissing Hand* (1993) by Audrey Penn

Reading these books aloud can lead to discussions geared toward better preparing young children to not only recognize but also begin to work through their emotions. Further, these books bring emotions and emotional outbursts to the center of teaching, challenging the silencing around such behaviors.

Further Considerations and Recommendations

Creating an inclusive environment where systemic injustices are named and troubled is integral to trauma-informed teaching. Critically examining children's literature that represents a variety of emotions, family structures, injustices experienced by students (such as deportation, incarceration of family members, homelessness, etc.), and other obstacles has been an integral component of my trauma-informed classroom. However, there are additional elements in conjunction with children's literature that can provide support within a classroom setting.

For example, creating a small quiet space in my classroom that students have access to throughout the day has proven to be helpful every year. This space is usually co-created with students, and we decide what to call it, the expectations for the space, and what it should be composed of. In previous years, it has been called the "peace corner," and students have decided to begin building it by adding calming visuals and other tools to reduce tensions and support relaxation; some of these tools are described in McConnico and colleagues' 2016 article, "A Framework for Trauma-Sensitive Schools." As the year progresses, we have conversations about what else to incorporate, and students always come up with ideas to meet their needs. One year some students suggested and benefited from noise-canceling headphones. Others enjoyed having scrap paper to tear up if they were feeling angry. Some asked for mandalas to color, which helped them become calm and focused. The peace corner also became a place where students wanted to read and write: they would ask for clipboards and take their work there with a partner. It became so popular that we needed to add a sand timer to help students keep track of time. Over the years, students have suggested and benefited from other tools and materials, such as sensory brushes, a rocking chair, books about feelings, and kinetic sand. In discussing what calmed them, how they self-regulated, students acknowledged negative emotions and made the space their own. I witnessed how students were able to self-regulate by asking me if they could go into the peace corner when they were feeling like they needed to center themselves. While these spaces can serve for self-regulation, it is essential to acknowledge—and to be open with the children—that the root of their trauma is not addressed by such palliative measures.

As we seek to foster trauma-informed teaching in classrooms and schools, it is important to understand that children work through their traumas in different ways. They may show different types of feelings or manifest particular behaviors in the classroom. As educators, it is our responsibility to help them work through their emotions and experiences. For Josiah, this continues to be a work in progress. As a classroom community, we continue to support him. What is most important is that as a collective we focus on strategies for love, care, and support—strategies that help all of us grow emotionally. Toward the end of the school year, Josiah no longer felt isolated because of his outbursts. Often he was the one asking other students if they needed a break or if they'd like company in the peace corner.

Having literature to help us facilitate these conversations is an essential part of every classroom. I have had difficulty finding resources that do not ignore the systemic roots and injustices of the issues children are experiencing, such as deportation, homelessness, parental incarceration, and extreme poverty, and I read trauma-informed resources critically, looking for solutions that are not merely mindfulness, yoga, or managing behaviors. As you set forth in your own journey to uphold your students' right to a trauma-informed classroom, here are a couple of resources that contain perspectives I have found helpful:

- "'Those Kids': Understanding Trauma-Informed Education" (2018) by Christina Torres
- "When Schools Cause Trauma" (2019) by Carrie Gaffney

I hope you will too!

References

Carello, J., & Butler, L. D. (2014). Potentially perilous pedagogies: Teaching trauma is not the same as trauma-informed teaching. *Journal of Trauma and Dissociation, 15*(2), 153–68.

Centers for Disease Control and Prevention. (2019). *Child abuse and neglect prevention* [Data file]. Retrieved from https://www.cdc.gov/violenceprevention/childabuseandneglect/index.html

Gaffney, C. (2019). When schools cause trauma. *Teaching Tolerance, 62*. Retrieved from https://www.tolerance.org/magazine/summer-2019/when-schools-cause-trauma

Ko, S. J., Ford, J. D., Kassam-Adams, N., Berkowitz, S. J., Wilson, C., Wong, M., Brymer, M. J., & Layne, C. M. (2008). Creating trauma-informed systems: Child welfare, education, first responders, health care, juvenile justice. *Professional Psychology: Research and Practice, 39*(4), 396–404.

McConnico, N., Boynton-Jarrett, R., Bailey, C., & Nandi, M. (2016). A framework for trauma-sensitive schools: Infusing trauma-informed practices into early childhood education systems. *Zero to Three, 36*(5), 36–44.

National Council of Teachers of English. (2018). *The students' right to read.* Retrieved from http://www2.ncte.org/statement/righttoreadguideline/

Taylor, R. D., Oberle, E., Durlak, J. A., & Weissberg, R. P. (2017). Promoting positive youth development through school-based social and emotional learning interventions: A meta-analysis of follow-up effects. *Child Development, 88*(4), 1156–71.

Torres, C. (2018, July 24). "Those kids": Understanding trauma-informed education. *Education Week.* Retrieved from https://blogs.edweek.org/teachers/intersection-culture-and-race-in-education/2018/07/those-kids-understanding-trauma-informed-education.html

Children's Books

Carle, E. (1995). *The very lonely firefly.* New York, NY: Philomel Books.

Chen, C-Y. (2004). *Guji guji.* La Jolla, CA: Kane/Miller.

Cooke, T. (2008). *Full, full, full of love* (P. Howard, Illus.). Cambridge, MA: Candlewick Press.

Cooper, F. (2013). *Max and the tag-along moon.* New York, NY: Philomel Books.

Fox, M. (1988). *Koala Lou.* San Diego, CA: Harcourt Brace.

Gunning, M. (2004). *A shelter in our car* (E. Pedlar, Illus.). San Francisco, CA: Children's Book Press.

Iwai, M. (2010). *Soup day.* New York, NY: Henry Holt.

Joosse, B. M. (1996). *I love you the purplest* (M. Whyte, Illus.). San Francisco, CA: Chronicle Books.

Keats, E. J. (1964). *Whistle for Willie*. New York, NY: Puffin Books.

Laguna, S. (2004). *Too loud Lily* (K. Argent, Illus.). New York, NY: Scholastic.

Lester, H. (2004). *Hurty feelings* (L. Munsinger, Illus.). Boston, MA: Houghton Mifflin.

Morales, Y. (2013). *Niño wrestles the world*. New York, NY: Roaring Book Press.

Moss, M. (2004). *Don't forget I love you* (A. Currey, Illus.). New York, NY: Dial Books for Young Readers.

Penn, A. (1993). *The kissing hand* (R. E. Harper and N. M. Leak, Illus.). Washington, DC: Child Welfare League of America.

Piper, W. (1976). *The little engine that could*. New York, NY: Platt & Munk.

Prestine, J. S. (2003). *Sometimes I feel awful* (V. Kylberg, Illus.). Columbus, OH: McGraw-Hill.

Schimel, L. (2011). *Let's go see Papá!* (A. M. Rivera, Illus.). Berkeley, CA: Groundwood Books/House of Anansi Press.

Silver, G. (2009). *Anh's anger* (C. Krömer, Illus.). Berkeley, CA: Plum Blossom Books.

Silver, G. (2011). *Steps and stones: An Anh's anger story* (C. Krömer, Illus.). Berkeley, CA: Plum Blossom Books.

Soetoro-Ng, M. (2011). *Ladder to the moon* (Y. Morales, Illus.). Somerville, MA: Candlewick Press.

Tonatiuh, D. (2010). *Dear primo: A letter to my cousin*. New York, NY: Abrams Books for Young Readers.

Viorst, J. (1987). *Alexander and the terrible, horrible, no good, very bad day* (R. Cruz, Illus.). New York, NY: Aladdin Books.

Willems, M. (2004). *Knuffle bunny: A cautionary tale*. New York, NY: Hyperion.

Woodson, J. (2002). *Visiting day* (J. Ransome, Illus.). New York, NY: Scholastic.

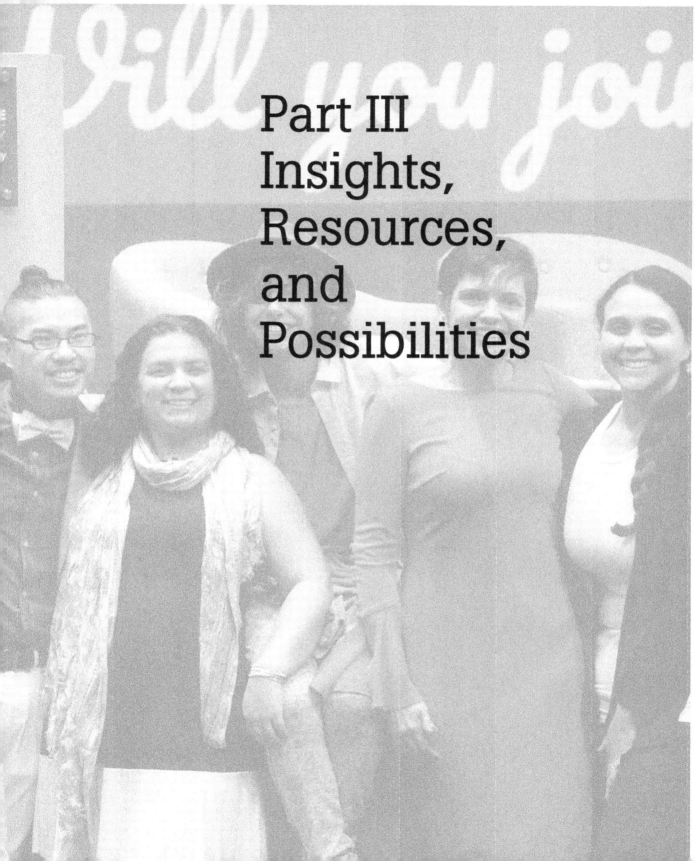

Part III
Insights,
Resources,
and
Possibilities

A Conversation with Jacqueline Woodson on Students' Rights to Read and Write

Mariana Souto-Manning

The following dialogic exchange took place between Mariana Souto-Manning and Jacqueline Woodson, bestselling author of more than two dozen award-winning books, including her *New York Times*–bestselling memoir, *Brown Girl Dreaming*, which received the National Book Award. It has been enriched by information on her website (Woodson, 2020) and TED Talk (Woodson, 2019).

As she reflects on her own life and experiences, Woodson makes visible the importance of upholding students' rights to read and write, as well as the importance of students having access to diverse books, books by and about people and communities of color.

Inspired by Paulo Freire (2000), we offer our conversation in dialogical format:

Dialogue is the encounter between . . . [humans] mediated by the world, in order to name the world. Hence, dialogue cannot occur between those who want to name the world and those who do not wish this naming—between those who deny others the right to speak their word and those whose right to speak has been denied them. Those who have been denied their primordial right to speak their word must first reclaim this right and prevent the continuation of this dehumanizing aggression. . . . It is in speaking their word that people, by naming the world, transform it. (p. 88)

Seeking to name the importance of diverse books and students' rights to read and write (inspired by the NCTE statements discussed in this book), we offer the following co-constructed text:

Mariana Souto-Manning: As an award-winning author of color writing about topics relevant to children and youth of color, were your rights to read and write supported in your early schooling?

Jacqueline Woodson: I grew up in Brooklyn in the '70s, and the teachers were all white and immensely dedicated to getting us to learn in the ways they'd been taught to teach us. There were the SRAs, weekly spelling and math tests, read-alouds from books of their choosing (usually the classics—Hans Christian Andersen, Robert Frost, Oscar Wilde, Truman Capote, etc.). In the classroom library there was a little bit of Langston Hughes and Eloise Greenfield sometimes and a lot of stuff by white writers. But I was encouraged to read—constantly. And I was being taught to write—both cursive and noncursive. I loved the physical act of writing, so learning the tool that I would need to create stories was important.

Mariana: So, were you encouraged to write from early on? In school and in other learning spaces?

Jacqueline: I wrote on everything and everywhere. I remember my uncle catching me writing my name in graffiti on the side of a building. (It was not pretty for me when my mother found out.) I wrote on paper bags and my shoes and denim binders. I chalked stories across sidewalks and penciled tiny tales in notebook margins. I loved and still love watching words flower into sentences and sentences blossom into stories.

Mariana: Wow! And now . . .

Jacqueline: Lots and lots of books later, I am still surprised when I walk into a bookstore and see my name on a book or when the phone rings and someone on the other end is telling me I've just won an award.

Mariana: Tell me about your schooling.

Jacqueline: Our class was a mix of Black, Latinx, German, Italian, and Irish kids throughout the lower school years. (As the neighborhood changed with white flight, so did our classroom makeup, but here I'm talking about those early years.) I don't think our teachers saw us as anything other than a group of students they were going to teach—again, what they knew how to teach. I was by far not an outstanding student, so as a result the teachers didn't see me as anything more than someone who'd need more work, different reading levels and reading groups, more yelling at. Did this nurture me as a writer?—yup.

Mariana: How?

Jacqueline: I think my writing has always been an act of resistance and a call to the other invisible young people like me in the classroom. What would have happened if there were different books, more conscious teaching, more visibility? I truly don't know. I think the fact that my brilliance wasn't honored and lauded let me kind of disappear inside my own dream without expectation. I saw my sister sail (she was literally the smartest kid in our neighborhood by far) and fall then rise again but by her own terms. The pressure on her to achieve became its own burden.

Mariana: Where did you access books about diverse people? And who encouraged you to develop as a reader?

Jacqueline: The public library supplied the books lacking in my classroom. My mother made sure we read constantly.

Mariana: What are the implications of your experiences for teaching all children—and in particular children of color—in ways that honor their brilliance and position them to become award-winning authors like you?

Jacqueline: I think having witnessed my academic experience in relation to my sister's, I would say that kids need to be seen and respected and taught—both at home and in the classroom. I think a balance between deep nurturing and serious structure is what I see working well.

Mariana: In your opinion, what is the role of books in upholding students' rights to read and write in their own language(s)?

Jacqueline: So important. More so, it's important that students have the books and stories they can fall in love with that will keep them running to reading . . . in their languages.

Mariana: Were these stories widely available in your schooling?

Jacqueline: No. Writing allowed me to create worlds where people could be seen and heard, where their experiences could be legitimized, and where my story, read or heard by another person, inspired something in them that became a connection between us, a conversation.

Mariana: Tell me about students' rights to read and write. What are your thoughts? Why are they important?

Jacqueline: All of us there were the descendants of a people who had not been allowed to learn to read or write. Imagine that: the danger of understanding how letters form words, the danger of words themselves, the danger of a literate people and their stories. . . . Among these almost-silenced people there were the ones who never learned to read. Their descendants, now generations out of enslavement, if well-off enough, had gone on to college, grad school, beyond.

Mariana: Within this historical context, is access to diverse stories and diverse books a privilege or a right? To books by and about people of color; those whose voices have been deliberately silenced?

Jacqueline: Well, sadly, I think now it's more a privilege, but [it] should definitely, without question, be a right. Sometimes we read to understand the future. Sometimes we read to understand the past. We read to get lost, to forget the hard times we're living in.

Mariana: Tell me more.

Jacqueline: Young people should have options, should be able to see themselves on the page, should know their narrative is part of a bigger narrative.

Mariana: And—what are teachers' responsibilities pertaining to this?

Jacqueline: I think it's important for teachers to educate themselves. There are so many ways to find great books. Classrooms aren't cookie cutters, and the teachers know best who their students are and what will appeal to them. If they don't, they should ask. There is also the responsibility of the teacher to be culturally aware: Who are these kids? What do they believe in? What is their family makeup, their rituals at home, their dreams? This all helps shape the classroom library.

Mariana: What kinds of books (and stories) are essential in today's class-rooms if we are to uphold young students' rights to read and write?

Jacqueline: All kinds.

Mariana: Why?

Jacqueline: Dr. Rudine Sims Bishop talks about the importance of mirrors and windows in literature, how children need to be able to see both reflections of themselves and windows into other worlds that they would have never imagined. I think more and more in this society, through fear, we're allowing our worlds to get smaller and smaller. I think that's a dangerous thing, but more than that, I think books can help assuage fear.

Mariana: You have been a spokesperson for the We Need Diverse Books campaign. Can you help teachers understand why we need diverse books? Whom do these books benefit? What is wrong with books that do not feature diverse characters?

Jacqueline: Diverse books benefit everyone—the young people who can see themselves on the pages and the ones who learn about someone new from the stories.

Mariana: Can you give me an example of how you learned from a "diverse book"?

Jacqueline: A great example for me is *El Deafo*—I feel like I learned so much about what it means to walk through the world as Cece Bell's characters did. It made me want a book from the perspective of someone deaf living inside a deaf community. Basically, it made me want more. I think that's what great books do.

Mariana: How do you hope the books you authored are used by elementary school teachers?

Jacqueline: I hope they're opening conversations about stuff that it's sometimes hard to talk about—race, economic class, sexuality, family, etc.

Mariana: Why?

Jacqueline: I think conversing is a step toward understanding one another, toward developing empathy. It can help us understand the past and together dream a better future.

References

Freire, P. (2000). *Pedagogy of the oppressed* (30th anniversary ed.). New York, NY: Bloomsbury Academic.

Woodson, J. (2019). What reading slowly taught me about writing. *TED Talk*. Retrieved from https://www.ted.com/talks/jacqueline_woodson_what_reading_slowly_taught_me_about_writing/transcript

Woodson, J. (2020). *My biography*. Retrieved from https://www.jacquelinewoodson.com/all-about-me/my-biography/

Protecting Your Students' Rights to Read and Write and Yours to Teach

Millie Davis
Former director, Intellectual Freedom Center, NCTE

> *Students have the right to read and write . . . from the earliest grades.*
> *Even before stringing symbols together to make meaning and decoding*
> *words written in books, young children are readers and writers in and*
> *of their worlds.*
> —Mariana Souto-Manning and Haeny S. Yoon,
> *Rethinking Early Literacies: Reading and Rewriting Worlds*

> *So, students' rights to write and read serve as a catalyst to think*
> *about . . . our teaching—not just curriculum, not just pedagogy, but the*
> *thinking, talking, and listening that we as ELA teachers do together*
> *with our students . . .*
> —Jonna Perrillo, NCTE Historian,
> "More Than the Right to Read"

As Mariana Souto-Manning, Haeny S. Yoon, and Jonna Perrillo suggest, your students have the rights to read, write, think, and talk, and you should plan your curriculum and make your text choices to foster these literacy practices. Once you've done that, though, do take proactive steps to protect these most important activities for your students and their learning. Then know where to turn if you're challenged.

While basing your curricular choices and classroom activities on the National Council of Teachers of English's *The Students' Right to Read* (2018) and *NCTE Beliefs about the Students' Right to Write* (2014), you should also be aware of and consider the rules and procedures your school district has in place and that, as an employee, you need to follow.

Know and Follow Your School Policies

In a 2016 survey of 3,180 K–12 NCTE *INBOX* readers, most of the 668 elementary teacher respondents didn't think selection policies were necessary because, they said, texts were selected for them and they felt that censorship was not a problem. Don't be among those who leave text selection to others or don't know about their district's policies.

Most school districts have school board policies governing how curricula and texts are chosen. While the board has to approve these selections, they often cede the selection process to teachers or administrative committees. There are also usually provisions for supplemental texts and for texts teachers choose independently. In addition, most school districts have policies on teaching controversial materials and on reconsidering texts. Only a very few districts have policies concerning student writing in general, but many insist that writing assignments adhere to the district or state standards. Most districts have state-mandated regulations for reporting certain types of student writing, such as writing that indicates students might harm themselves or others. You'll usually find policies on the district website under "school board" and "school board policies" and then under "curriculum" and/or "instruction." You may have to dig a bit, but do familiarize yourself with these policies—for two reasons. First, know the policy so you can follow it in the selection of materials and methods for your classroom and the assignment of writing. Second, know the policy so you can at least notice where and when it's not being followed—for example, if a family or community member goes straight to a school board meeting to complain about a text or method or assignment you're using in your class instead of coming to you first. See the model procedure spelled out in *The Students' Right to Read*. (Note that I use "family members" to mean immediate and extended family members as well as guardians.)

Keeping People Informed and Building Buy-In

Beyond knowing the district policies, make sure to keep others in the loop about how you are teaching reading and writing, especially if you're including activities and texts that some may find controversial. Open your door and share with your colleagues, the principal, and family and community members about *what you're doing in your class, why, and how students are learning from it.* You don't need to be super specific. Something important to remember, as Emily Knox's *Book Banning in 21st Century America* (2015) points out, is that challengers often just want to be heard, and they don't really understand the reading or writing processes as we do. So help them to understand.

What Others May Not Know about How We Teach Our Students

Celia Genishi and Anne Haas Dyson (2009) note:

> In the early 21st century we seem to be stuck in a time warp in which children who embody certain kinds of diversity have become the problem, and standardization has become the "fix. . . . [R]ecently set policy related to language and literacy insist[s] that children and teachers in schools and centers live with a disconnect, with this educational paradox: There is a profusion of human diversity in our schools and an astonishingly narrow offering of curricula. (p. 10)

This became particularly the case for children from minoritized backgrounds who, albeit not the numeric minority, are treated in ways that marginalize their values, experiences, and knowledges. So it's critical to explain to stakeholders a new way of working that supports students' cultural identities and diversity, maybe as Alison Lanza does in her chapter:

> Roots and wings: the overall objective each year for my teaching practice. Having children honor their roots and their cultural identity by simply holding up a mirror and letting them see their reflection as powerful creates a sense of courage and the fortitude to use their metaphorical wings to take risks and persevere in this short life.

James S. Chisholm and Kathryn F. Whitmore, authors of *Reading Challenging Texts: Layering Literacies through the Arts* (2018), point out that the more ways we look at literature, the more we involve ourselves in literature, the more we learn about it, ourselves, and our community. They:

> recognize that to decide to read such literature with students is an act of professional courage. Every student has the right to read and the "freedom to explore ideas and pursue truth whenever and however they wish" (National Council of Teachers of English, 2018). Furthermore, young people have the right to see themselves and others in the literature they read—and to be able to step in and out of those vicarious experiences. And . . . students deserve opportunities to question, enjoy, challenge, and learn about and from the literature they read. (p. 11)

Teaching like this requires courage because, as they also acknowledge:

> Some adults ascribe to and express a discourse of innocence, which references the desire that children and adolescents be kept from knowing about emotionally troubling content. These well-meaning adults intend to protect young learners and assume

they aren't able to understand or engage with challenging topics. The discourse of innocence can be used as a primary mechanism of regulation by school administrators, teachers, and families, and serves as a rationale for censoring instructional materials that disrupt the status quo. (pp. 9–10)

But sometimes stakeholders don't listen, and even the best laid plans occasionally go awry.

What to Do When Challenges Arise

If the challenge comes and you need help, contact NCTE through the Intellectual Freedom Center (http://www2.ncte.org/resources/ncte-intellectual-freedom-center/). Use the Report a Censorship Challenge incident form (https://secure.ncte.org/forms/reportcensorship) or email intellectualfreedom@ncte.org.

While a variety of organizations deal with challenges to reading and writing in schools, they are not all equal in terms of the help and insight they can provide, their methods for doing so, and *their understandings of reading and writing in terms of English language arts pedagogy, curriculum, and instruction.* Many resource books about censorship provide lists of organizations that work with challenges, but they don't do more than that—leaving a person who needs help to pick from the list at random.

Chutzpa or not, we at NCTE are the best "door" for educators to walk through when they have a problem. We understand reading and writing in terms of English language arts pedagogy, curriculum, and instruction. We know and regularly work with all the other First Amendment organizations. We rarely try to solve the problem alone but do so with those organizations whose expertise can help.

NCTE bases its responses to challenges on:

- procedures—what the district policies say about curriculum, instruction, and texts;
- whether the procedures have been followed;
- the value of the text—we have ready-made, adaptable rationales for hundreds of books and a form to use to create your own rationale; and most important,
- NCTE beliefs about good pedagogy, curriculum, and instruction in English language arts.

We keep our interactions with teachers who have been challenged private unless the challenge is already public knowledge because it's been broadcast in the media. Two examples:

- When *March, Books 1–3* by John Lewis, Andrew Aydin, and Nate Powell were challenged in an elementary classroom, removed, and the teacher who offered them to students suspended, NCTE joined the National Coalition Against Censorship (NCAC) and nine other free speech organizations in writing the superintendent to restore the book and reinstate the teacher.

- NCTE joined NCAC and seven other free speech organizations to defend the book *I Am Jazz* by Jessica Herthel and Jazz Jennings when the Liberty Counsel threatened a lawsuit against the Mount Horeb, Wisconsin, school district to prevent readings of the book in its Primary Center (https://www.scribd.com/document/292962251/NCAC-Letter-Liberty-Counsel-and-I-am-Jazz). Although the district cancelled the reading, a philanthropist in town partnered with the local library to host a reading that drew 600 attendees! A YouTube video was made about the challenge (https://www.youtube.com/watch?v=IY-kQtI2hY4), and the SAGA 6, the students and advisors who worked to save the reading, received an Honorable Mention for NCTE's 2017 Intellectual Freedom Award.

It would be great if discussions with family or community members could always be conducted gently and instructively. You can first try listening to objecting family or community members carefully and attentively, and then ask them to take a moment, take the high view, and state their feelings about the text and their student reading it or the topic the class is studying. No promises here, but this first approach is worth a try. And if objectors still feel they must challenge the text, you might offer their students an alternative text. Possibly you could have all students work in groups, each with a different text or topic, with some texts or topics considered "safer" than others by potential challengers.

Often challengers react to parts of a text (e.g., an incident on a certain page of the book, or some bit of language, as in *March* or *Maniac Magee*), to something they don't approve of and don't want their student or any student to read about (e.g., another culture in the multicultural and fractured fairy tales Carmen Llerena mentions in her chapter, sexuality in *I Am Jazz*, or magic in the Harry Potter books), or to something they've seen in a movie, read about in an article, or heard on the news about the book (e.g., the magic and some language in the film version of *A Wrinkle in Time* or two male penguins raising an egg together in *And Tango Makes Three* and the book's frequent appearance on the ALA List of Challenged Books). It's important to remind family and community members that we teach whole texts and not bowdlerized parts, that their children are likely much stronger and wiser than they give them credit for, and that children need and benefit from books that family or community members often object to (e.g., *The Watsons Go to Birmingham* or *Where the Sidewalk Ends*).

To educate, we often teach controversial materials. In fact, the Supreme Court case *Island Trees Union Free School District v. Pico* (1982), which NCTE joined in amicus curiae, established that minors do have First Amendment rights in schools, including the right to receive information, even controversial information. That means that a text used in class need not agree with the challenger's beliefs (e.g., *Attack of the Mutant Underwear, Number the Stars, Esperanza Rising, The Giver*) and that students can write on and discuss a wide variety of issues about which there is disagreement. Note that the *Monteiro v. The Tempe Union High School District* decision (1998) recognized the First Amendment right of students to read books selected for their "legitimate educational value," even if offensive to some family or community members and students.

Despite our efforts, challenges may happen. The first step is to keep your head. Then contact the NCTE Intellectual Freedom Center (http://www2.ncte .org/resources/ncte-intellectual-freedom-center/), where you can explain the situation and be heard, ask questions, receive resources, and walk through some possibilities for handling the challenge.

Sometimes we'll want to involve other organizations. They include the following:

- National Coalition Against Censorship (http://ncac.org/report-censorship-page). NCTE is a member of the Coalition. NCAC supports the "freedom to explore, the freedom to think, [and] the freedom to create," and, through their Kids' Right to Read Center, deals with a wide variety of challenges to classroom materials and student rights. Most challenges result in a letter to the school board—NCTE is often a signatory on these. NCAC also deals with other sorts of challenges, such as the display of artwork in a wide variety of venues. They have staff with legal expertise.

- American Library Association (http://www.ala.org/aboutala/offices/oif). ALA's Office of Intellectual Freedom focuses on challenges to libraries in schools and communities. It produces the annual list of most challenged books and was the initiator of Banned Books Week (http://www.banned booksweek.org/, where you can also find resources). It has staff with legal expertise and a nationwide network of librarians who report on challenges in their areas. NCTE works with ALA on library challenges and occasionally signs onto their letters; ALA occasionally signs onto NCAC letters.

- Comic Book Legal Defense Fund (http://cbldf.org/resources/). CBLDF supports intellectual freedom by making great resources available on graphic novels and comic books, specifically working with challenges to comics or graphic novels, and by signing onto letters produced by NCAC and occasionally writing press releases and letters of their own.

- Your local teachers' union can help you should the challenge rise to a personnel issue, such as suspension or insubordination.

- American Civil Liberties Union (https://www.aclu.org/defending-our-rights). ACLU is a great organization to have on your side if you feel your civil liberties have been tampered with. NCTE and NCAC have worked with ACLU in challenge cases that have become political, as well as side by side with them as we protect the text or teaching methodology, and they protect the teacher. They are quite knowledgeable about personal freedoms and local and state education politics.

- American Booksellers for Free Expression (http://www.bookweb.org/abfe) is a strong supporter of free expression in books. They are often signatories onto the NCAC letters.

- Authors Guild (https://www.authorsguild.org/) supports working writers and their works. They write letters in defense of authors' books and often sign onto NCAC letters.

- Society of Children's Book Writers and Illustrators (https://www.scbwi.org/) supports those individuals writing and illustrating for children and young adults in the fields of children's literature, magazines, film, television, and multimedia. They write letters in support of children's book authors and illustrators and are often signatories to NCAC letters.

- PEN America Children's/Young Adult Book Authors Committee (https://pen.org/childrensyoung-adult-book-authors-committee/) supports writers and librarians whose books have been banned or challenged. They write their own letters and commentaries and often sign onto NCAC letters.

Helpful NCTE Position Statements and Resources

And finally, here are some useful NCTE resources to consult when facing a text challenge:

- *The Students' Right to Read* (http://www2.ncte.org/statement/rightto readguideline/)

- *NCTE Beliefs about the Students' Right to Write* (http://www2.ncte.org/statement/students-right-to-write/)

- *Guidelines for Selection of Materials in English Language Arts Programs* (http://www2.ncte.org/statement/material-selection-ela/)

- *Rationales for Classroom Texts* (http://www.ncte.org/action/anti-censorship/rationales)

- *Guidelines for Dealing with Censorship of Instructional Materials* (http://www2.ncte.org/statement/censorshipofnonprint/)

- *Statement on Classroom Libraries* (http://www2.ncte.org/statement/classroom-libraries/)

- *NCTE Position Statement Regarding Rating or "Red-Flagging" Books* (http://www2.ncte.org/statement/rating-books/)

- *Statement on Academic Freedom (Revised)* (http://www2.ncte.org/statement/academic-freedom/)
- *Statement on Censorship and Professional Guidelines* (http://www2.ncte.org/statement/censorshipprofguide/)
- *Resolution on the Need for Diverse Children's and Young Adult Books* (http://www2.ncte.org/statement/diverse-books/)
- *Supporting Linguistically and Culturally Diverse Learners in English Education* (http://www2.ncte.org/statement/diverselearnersinee/)

References

Chisholm, J. S., & Whitmore, K. F. (2018). *Reading challenging texts: Layering literacies through the arts*. New York, NY, and Urbana, IL: Routledge and National Council of Teachers of English.

Genishi, C., & Dyson, A. H. (2009). *Children, language, and literacy: Diverse learners in diverse times*. New York, NY, and Washington, DC: Teachers College Press and National Association for the Education of Young Children.

Island Trees School District v. Pico, 457 U.S. 853 (1982).

Knox, E. J. M. (2015). *Book banning in 21st-century America*. Lanham, MD: Rowman & Littlefield.

Monteiro v. The Tempe Union High School District, 158 F. 3d 1022 (9th Ct. App. 1998).

National Council of Teachers of English. (2014). *NCTE beliefs about the students' right to write*. Retrieved from http://www2.ncte.org/statement/students-right-to-write/

National Council of Teachers of English. (2018). *The students' right to read*. Retrieved from http://www2.ncte.org/statement/righttoreadguideline/

Perrillo, J. (2017, September 17). More than the right to read. *Literacy & NCTE* [Blog]. Retrieved from http://www2.ncte.org/blog/2017/09/more-than-the-right-to-read/

Souto-Manning, M. and Yoon, H. S. (2018). *Rethinking early literacies: Reading and rewriting worlds*. Abingdon, UK: Routledge.

Chapter Nine

In the Pursuit of Justice: On the Rights to Read and Write as Human Rights

Mariana Souto-Manning, with Benelly Álvarez, Billy Fong, Alison Lanza, Carmen Lugo Llerena, Karina Malik, Jessica Martell, Emme Pelosi, and Patty Pión

So what?" and "What's next?" These are some of the questions Benelly Álvarez, Billy Fong, Alison Lanza, Carmen Lugo Llerena, Karina Malik, Jessica Martell, Patty Pión, Emma Pelosi, and Mariana Souto-Manning took up as we met over the course of a year. Three additional teachers joined us but didn't write chapters for this book, as one of them had just given birth (Abigail Salas Maguire, often joined by her little one, an honorary member of our learning community); one had started a teaching position in a new school (Inés Zanotti); and one was a teacher of toddlers, thus teaching outside the scope of the elementary grades (Tara Lencl). We started getting together after the election of the forty-fifth president of the United States. Our meetings were prompted by texts Mariana received immediately after the election results were released by the US media. Some of the texts (or sections of texts) read:

"What now?"

"I feel like I lied to my kids. I taught them that bullies don't prevail. How do I face them?"

"This sure is a blow."

"What do I tell my students with disabilities??? That Americans think it's okay for them to be mocked?" [referring to how Trump mocked a *New York Times* reporter with a disability]

Although not all of our group members sent Mariana texts, they all went on to teach the day after the election. Benelly, Billy, Alison, Carmen, Karina, Jessica, Patty, Emma, Abby, Inés, and Tara faced students who cried. They saw students throw up. Some students expressed fear that their parents would be deported. Some students didn't come to school at all. Others expressed great anxiety over fear of separation from their parents or caregivers. The fear and anxiety experienced by a number of students was palpable. Teachers also witnessed girls declare: "When I grow up, I'm gonna be president."

This moment in history reminded us that our students' rights were under attack. So we got together as a community to talk about how to protect our students' rights when our rights—as women, as immigrants, as gay people, as people with disabilities—were under attack. In our first meeting, we spent more than two hours answering the questions "Who am I?" and "Why am I here?" We got to know one another—and built a community that was at once vulnerable and powerful. Although we met on Friday afternoons (often 4:00–7:00 p.m. at Teachers College, Columbia University), at the end of our work weeks, we left our meetings reenergized and reaffirmed; our collective was a site where we developed a renewed sense of purpose. Although some of us had commutes that lasted close to two hours after our meetings, it wasn't uncommon for messages of gratitude to be sent to the group following our meetings, messages that expressed sentiments such as "I wanted to reach out and let y'all know that I appreciated yesterday's meeting very much. More than a meeting, it served as a healing circle that I was unaware I needed."

Our conversations often started with a scenario from one of our classrooms, such as how students felt disengaged as a result of a Eurocentric reading curriculum, or students' fears of speaking Spanish because doing so might somehow signal that they either didn't belong in the United States or that they weren't smart. Sometimes we began with an event from the news that had affected their students. For example, we talked about immigration and the imprisonment of migrant children held in concentration camps by the US government. We talked about how white people were routinely calling police on Black people who were picnicking, visiting colleges, and selling water. We talked about the apparent "disposability of Black lives" (Hill, 2016). We problematized the roots of these issues and dialogued. We talked, we cried, we were there for each other. We problem-solved together and plotted courses of action.

We engaged in a process inspired by Freirean culture circles (Freire, 1970; Souto-Manning, 2010), and physically we always met in circles to break the hierarchies set up by typical classroom arrangements. Individually, we undertook thematic investigations, reading our worlds and identifying issues of oppression. Then, together, as we shared some of our thematic investigations, we identified generative themes that resonated with the entire community. We codified these themes into stories, scenarios, and dilemmas, which were then dialogically problematized. In problem posing, we undertook a process whereby we sought to understand the history and roots of the issues at hand. As we dialogued and considered multiple voices and perspectives, we came to more in-depth and nuanced understandings of the issues. Once we reached a better understanding of the issue—acknowledging and considering its history—we sought to foster justice by problem solving and devising plans of action—collectively and individually— with the potential to interrupt injustice and foster justice, transformatively. The process was recursive and not as linear as described here. Our work is best captured by the graphic in Figure 9.1.

So, in this concluding chapter, we undertake a similar process. Identifying students' rights as a generative theme, as practiced by the members of our culture circle community, we take you on a journey that highlights some of our learnings. In problematizing students' rights to read and write (and rights in general), we invite you to consider the difference between the concept of a right and that of a privilege, and to link students' rights to our responsibility as teachers to uphold these rights. We thus reject reading and writing as privileges, and redefine reading and writing as rights. That is, instead of positioning reading and writing as obligations or as privileges, we propose that we must unequivocally reposition them as rights, which must be upheld by schools and schooling.

Figure 9.1. The critical cycle (adapted from Souto-Manning, 2019).

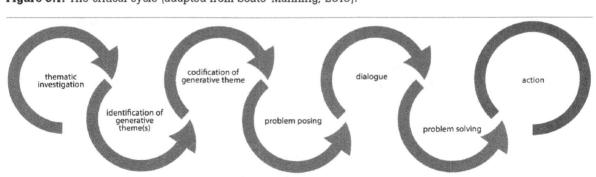

Drawing on the practices showcased in Part II and on the brilliance of the teachers with whom we have worked for the past few years and who have written here about their teaching practices that uphold students' rights to read, to write, and to speak their own language, we underscore the need to (re)center the teaching of reading and writing on the lives, practices, values, and experiences of minoritized individuals and communities—those who, even when numerically the majority, continue to be positioned as inferior to, or lesser than, the dominant population (McCarty, 2002). Teaching that upholds students' rights must center students, families, and communities—not as a choice, not as an option, but as an imperative.

We conclude with an invitation to approach the teaching of reading and writing from a students' rights perspective. And while this is an invitation, we want to frame this invitation within the context of our students' rights—not privileges—to read, write, and talk. In doing so, we propose that it is our responsibility to engage in teaching that defends, upholds, cultivates, and extends their rights as a matter of freedom. We do so because we understand that practices cannot be simplistically imported and exported (Freire, 1998). We believe that freedom is predicated on the right to representation and linguistic pluralism. Students need to see and hear themselves, their families, and their communities in the materials they read—and they must see the diversities within the society in which they live. They must also have the right to write, to author themselves, making use of their sophisticated languaging repertoires, through a variety of tools, such as the visual autobiographies in Benelly's fourth grade or the portraits and letters in Alison's second-grade class.

We do not believe in simple, foolproof recipes for teaching—even under the guise of justice. After all, teaching is contextualized and situated. Teaching is both a matter of humanity and of freedom. It is a political endeavor. In inviting you to reimagine or extend your own practice, we propose that the examples, resources, approaches, and tools showcased in Part II can shed light onto what is possible.

Problematizing Rights, Considering Privileges and Responsibilities

Rights matter. "The right to read [is a right] like all rights guaranteed or implied within our constitutional tradition" (NCTE, 2018, p. x). This is a seemingly simple statement. But what do we mean by "rights"? What do these rights encompass? Isn't reading a "choice book" a privilege? And what is our responsibility as educators to ensure that these rights are upheld in spite of testing pressures and curricular mandates? These are important questions if we are to uphold and honor our students' rights to read and write in our classrooms and schools. Additionally, to secure our students' rights, we must affirm inclusive teaching that fosters multiple ways of reading, writing, and talking.

As we consider the meanings of *right, privilege,* and *responsibility,* we draw on the *Merriam-Webster* dictionary (n.d.), which defines them this way:

Right (noun): "something that a person is or should be morally or legally allowed to have, get, or do."

Privilege (noun): "granted as a peculiar benefit, advantage, or favor."

Responsibility (noun): "the state of being the person who caused something to happen; a duty or task that you are required or expected to do; something that you should do because it is morally right, legally required, etc."

These three concepts are essential as we consider what it means to defend and uphold students' rights to read, to write, and to their own language in our classrooms. After all, while reading and writing are forwarded as "rights" by NCTE, they may in fact be enacted as privileges in many classrooms—especially when these rights pertain to student choice in, and access to, diverse reading materials, multiple modes of authoring, and writing opportunities.

As *The Students' Right to Read* explicates, "One of the foundations of a democratic society is the individual's right to read, and also the individual's right to freely choose what they would like to read. This right is based on an assumption that the educated possess judgment and understanding and can be trusted with the determination of their own actions" (NCTE, 2018, p. x). Interestingly, while educators are more comfortable with student choice in reading in the upper grades (middle and high school), young children are often framed as incapable and/or as unready. As such, we educators rationalize making choices for them—or limiting their choices by deeming certain books to be "inappropriate."

The NCTE statement proposes that it is essential to understand that it is our responsibility as teachers to work to protect and uphold our students' rights to read and write. To have a responsibility means to be "answerable or accountable for something within one's power, control, or management" (Searcy, 2011). And while NCTE's statements affirm that students have the rights to read and write, such rights often come under threat as the pressures explored in Part I mount.

For example, it is not uncommon to hear from teachers, "You can read a choice book once you've read your leveled book." As a result, students come to devalue their voices. They say things like "This book doesn't count" or "This is not a school book." We educators risk stripping our students of their right to read (NCTE, 2018). Specifically, recasting reading choice as a privilege is likely to disenfranchise minoritized children, families, and communities. After all, the overwhelming majority of published children's books are by and about white people (as clarified in Part I). Limiting choice in students' reading and writing is likely to limit the possibilities for what counts as reading and what is regarded as writing to those forms that are dominant in society.

Additionally, our responsibility to uphold students' rights must be understood within the history of people of color being denied the rights to read and write and being denied the right to their own language(s). Enslaved Africans, for example, were denied the right to read (Davis, 1981). Likewise, throughout history, minoritized communities have been denied the right to speak their own language. Examples include enslaved Africans being separated by language so they couldn't communicate with one another, and the assertion of English as the dominant language in the Hawaiian islands. Indigenous languages were threatened, and some even eradicated, via forced processes of assimilation. Spanish continues to come under attack in the United States, and to signal academic ineptitude or limited intellect (e.g., *Hermino Hernandez v. Driscoll CISD*, 1957). African American Language is persistently attacked by racist comments, which deem it to be "broken" or "lazy" English.

In light of these and other persistent attacks rooted in myths of the (purported) superiority of dominant American English and in the false idea of the existence of a standard language, NCTE took a clear stand for justice through its Conference on College Composition and Communication (CCCC) and adopted the following resolution in 1974:

> We affirm the students' right to their own patterns and varieties of language—the dialects of their nurture or whatever dialects in which they find their own identity and style. Language scholars long ago denied that the myth of a standard American dialect has any validity. The claim that any one dialect is unacceptable amounts to an attempt of one social group to exert its dominance over another. . . . A nation proud of its diverse heritage and its cultural and racial variety will preserve its heritage of dialects. We affirm strongly that teachers must have the experiences and training that will enable them to respect diversity and uphold the right of students to their own language.

We see *Students' Right to Their Own Language* as essential to upholding, protecting, and promoting our students' rights to read and write. This is visible, for example, in the chapters authored by Benelly Álvarez and by Patty Pión and Emma Pelosi. It is also visible and modeled in Alison Lanza's prose and in her students' poetry.

Historically Contextualizing the Rights to Read and Write

History matters. It is important to historically contextualize the rights to read and write. While we do not undertake a full exploration of the long history of denying communities of color the rights to read, to write, and to their own languages, we offer here a brief contextualization as a way of helping us better understand our responsibilities to uphold our students' rights to read and write as a matter of justice. After all, it was not too long ago that denying the rights to read and write were sanctioned forms of oppression. For many enslaved Africans, "the ability to read meant freedom" (Division of Rare and Manuscript Collections, 2002).

As Apple (2009) documented, throughout history, there have been "many murderous prohibitions against teaching slaves of African descent to read in the United States and the Caribbean. Thus, for example, in slave-holding Jamaica, the idea of literate 'slaves' was dangerous and offensive to most whites" (p. xii). In the United States:

> every case of literacy on the part of enslaved Africans challenged Enlightenment ideas about African American deficiency and some compelling cases actually demanded an affidavit from other Whites since the capacity to reason in a written form violated the expectation of African American failure. (Walker, 2009, p. xvi)

With the exceptions of Maryland and Kentucky, all Southern states had antiliteracy laws that restricted the education of enslaved human beings, who at the time were regarded as property (Davis, 1981). And, as Vanessa Siddle Walker (2009) explained: "If Africans, thus, did not record their history in writing, their failure could be equated, as far as the Europeans were concerned, with the failure of African Americans to achieve humanity" (p. xv). From this perspective, the right to write was a matter of existence and a matter of humanity. It means that writing rights are human rights. When understood as such, our responsibility to support students' right to write outweighs any mandates or pressures that may constrain our teaching or restrict the materials available to us and to our students.

It is within this context that we seek to make "visible the connections between literacy and Black empowerment that are sometimes masked in traditional histories" (Walker, 2009, p. xvii). After all, "enslaved African Americans . . . [becoming] the conduits through which reasoned language could emerge in written form challenged the White supremacy that formed the very foundations upon which the country was being built" (p. xvi). Thus, the right to literacy—to read, to write, to speak in one's language—is central to the construction of a more just world, a world where whiteness and Eurocentrism are challenged and decentered. Eurocentrism reflects a tendency to interpret the world according to European-dominant values and experiences, centering whiteness.

From Reconstruction (dating from 1863) to the Civil Rights Movement (1950s and 1960s), literacy was a key "ingredient for freedom" (Walker, 2009, p. xvii)—for adults and children alike. The importance of literacy in the 1950s is illustrated in the perspective of a child in the *Goin' Someplace Special* (2001) by Patricia McKissack, a realistic fictional portrayal of her own experiences in the segregated South. McKissack reminds us that "reading is the doorway to freedom" (Author's Note). Regarding literacy as essential to freedom, we thus reframe the rights to read, to write, and to speak one's own language as human rights.

The Responsibility to (Re)Center Literacy on the Lives, Legacies, and Values of Minoritized Communities

As we come to understand the rights to read (NCTE, 2018), to write (NCTE, 2014), and to speak one's own languages (CCCC, 1974) as human rights, we must understand that such rights run counter to the traditional imposition of "Eurocentric realities as universal, i.e., that which is white is presented as applied to the human condition in general, while that which is non-white is viewed as group-specific and therefore not human" (Asante, 1991, p. 172). Thus, Eurocentrism offers a threat to students' rights to read and write. This means that our teaching and the materials we employ must decenter whiteness and center the lives, legacies, and values of minoritized communities of color. This is the common thread in the chapters that constitute Part II of this book. To uphold students' rights, we must make this our responsibility.

In choosing to center potentially controversial texts in their fourth-grade classroom, for example, Jessica Martell and Billy Fong defended their students' rights to explore and wrestle with racism and homophobia as entangled forms of bigotry. In doing so, they did not impose their perspectives, but instead asked questions and offered texts for their students to consider. That is, they "avoid[ed] indoctrination because of personal beliefs and . . . [were] respectful of" their students' ideas orally and in writing (NCTE, 2014, p. xix). They engaged with reading and writing as pathways to problematizing and deconstructing stereotypes—which, according to Adichie (2009), are fostered when one single story becomes the only story about a community. In this way, they were able to foster their students' development as readers and writers while also honoring their development as everyday activists.

Disrupting a Eurocentric reading curriculum (E. D. Hirsch's Core Knowledge), rooted in the belief that multicultural education should not be allowed to "supplant or interfere with our schools' responsibility to ensure our children's mastery of American literate culture" (Hirsch, 1987, p. 18), Carmen Llerena provided her students with textual counternarratives in order to uphold their rights to read and write. In fact, Carmen expanded NCTE's statement on students' right to write to encompass their right to author multimodally—through art, performance, and story writing. While many teachers prioritize family and community cultures, Carmen prioritized childhood cultures, or peer cultures (Souto-Manning & Yoon, 2018). She centered her students' voices, perspectives, and lives, even as the mandated reading curriculum marginalized them.

Seeking to center the voices, experiences, languaging practices, and names of her mostly Latinx fourth graders in a New York City dual language classroom, Benelly Álvarez chose literature by and about Latinx individuals and communities. Reading Alma Flor Ada's books *Nacer Bailando* (2011) and *Me Llamo María Isabel*

(1993), she invited her students to proudly explore and come to better understand their identities through a visual autobiography. Centering Spanishes and Latinx perspectives and stories, she upheld students' rights to their identities and languaging practices in and through her teaching. In doing so, she decentered Eurocentric curricular perspectives and fostered a humanizing pedagogy that privileged her students' rights to read, write, and talk.

Karina Malik prioritized her first-grade students' experiences with trauma as she carefully selected books that would serve as windows, mirrors, and sliding glass doors (Bishop, 1990). Understanding the need to select literature for a variety of purposes (NCTE, 2018), Karina engaged in teaching that allowed children to understand trauma while not blaming them for behaviors related to their experiences with trauma. In addition, she engaged her students in writing their emotions on an emotion wall, labeling abstract concepts and enacting the belief that "[t]he expression of ideas without fear of censorship is a fundamental right" (NCTE, 2014, p. xix). Further, she understood how "[w]ords are a powerful tool of expression, a means to clarify, explore, inquire, and learn as well as a way to record present moments," with the potential to benefit the future of a community (NCTE, 2014, p. xix). Thus, she engaged in upholding her students' rights to read and write in her classroom, humanizing their experiences with trauma in the process.

Patty Pión and Emma Pelosi explained how they engaged their second-grade students in reading their own languaging practices, exploring issues pertaining to linguistic hierarchies. Their chapter explores how

> education is an effort to improve the quality of choices open to all students. But to deny the freedom of choice in fear that it may be unwisely used is to destroy the freedom itself. For this reason, [Emma and Patty] respect[ed] the right of individuals to be selective in their own reading. (NCTE, 2018, p. x)

They engaged their students in a critical exploration of the linguistic resources available to them while troubling their assumption that dominant American English was the preferred and more highly valued language. While they did not censor the use of English in their classroom, they engaged their students in critiquing their own use of English as a purportedly superior language. They explored the difference between examining, critiquing, and censoring languaging practices (NCTE, 2018), considering questions such as:

- Which languages are represented in the books in our classroom library?
- Which languages are represented in the books in the school library?
- What does this tell you?

In fact, this is one of the dialogues their classroom community undertook. They documented from a critical perspective the subtractive representation of Latinx in the books of their classroom library and of their entire school. Such books serve as tools for critically educating and centering the communicative strengths of Latinx children, families, and communities. In doing so, they denounced the lack of representation they found as they audited books and simultaneously worked to uphold students' right to freedom in and through reading, expanding the choices available to them by working to add books by and about Latinx people to these libraries.

Finally, Alison Lanza prioritized her students' realization of their identities. With the understanding that "teachers . . . may use different texts for different purposes . . . [and that t]he criteria for choosing a work to be read by an entire class are somewhat different from the criteria for choosing works to be read by small groups" (NCTE, 2018, p. x), Alison selected books that centered and honored multiple identities. In her second-grade classroom, she selected *Looking Like Me* (2009) by Walter Dean Myers; in her fourth-grade classroom, she chose *The Best Part of Me* (2002) by Wendy Ewald. She understood that the right to read invariably encompasses the right to representation. And the books she selected for whole-class engagements represented many of her students' experiences; they could see themselves in these books. For some, the books served as mirrors and validated their experiences (Bishop, 1990); for others, the books provided insights into others' experiences. Alison created ways for her students to express their ideas without fear of censorship or judgment, a key belief espoused by NCTE (2014). In using portraiture and poetry, she ensured that her students had powerful tools to express who they were. She thus freed her students from past ideas and labels that deemed them to be inadequate and/or not good enough. She created expansive spaces where students could revision and author their identities in positive ways, ways that acknowledged their power creatively (NCTE, 2014).

These are just some of the ways in which the teachers whose practices, voices, and classes are included in this book defended their students' rights to read (NCTE, 2018), to write (NCTE, 2014), and to speak their own language (CCCC, 1974), thereby honoring the full humanity of their students. We hope that as you read and reflect on how they brought these principles to their practice, you start to consider how you might engage in reimagining your classroom, expanding your practice, purposefully and intentionally prioritizing your students' rights to read, write, and speak in ways that sustain their histories, experiences, practices, and identities.

An Invitation

Together with the authors of the chapters in Parts II and III of this book, I invite you to embrace the responsibility to uphold students' rights in and through your teaching. Doing so is not truly an option; it is our responsibility. After all, our students' rights to read (NCTE, 2018), to write (NCTE, 2014), and to speak their own language (CCCC, 1974) are not privileges. These rights are not to be "granted as a peculiar benefit, advantage, or favor" (Privilege, n.d.). They are the rights of ALL of our students, and as such, they must be upheld. This is our job.

Embracing such a responsibility entails ongoing work. It entails troubling pressures and restrictive curricular mandates, and instead defending choice, the ability to explore and engage with controversial texts, and upholding a view of our students as capable agents. As a song written in honor of Civil Rights activist Ella Baker reminds us, "We who believe in freedom cannot rest."

Together, we conclude with a reminder and an invitation to action. As educators committed to fostering justice in and through our teaching, we teachers must continue to defend our students' rights as learners and as human beings. This requires understanding that literacies are plural. Literacies are the practice of freedom (hooks, 1994). It is imperative that we commit to interrupting the harm inflicted on communities of color by narrow and restrictive conceptualizations of what counts as literacy. Further, it is of utmost importance that we teach in the pursuit of justice, upholding students' rights to their own language and literacy practices as human rights. We know this is a big responsibility, but it is one that is central to our profession. So, as members of a learning collective—what some call professional learning communities—we invite you to take on this work collectively. Upholding our students' rights is our responsibility as professionals and, collectively, as a profession. And we have NCTE to support us. We sincerely hope you will accept our invitation to join us in this work—and bring these important NCTE principles to practice in your classroom!

References

Adichie, C. N. (2009). *The danger of a single story*. TED Global. Retrieved from http://www.ted.com/talks/chimamanda_adichie_the_danger_of_a_single_story.html

Apple, M. W. (2009). Series editor introduction. In M. T. Fisher, *Black literate lives: Historical and contemporary perspectives* (pp. ix–xii). New York, NY: Routledge.

Asante, M. K. (1991). The Afrocentric idea in education. *Journal of Negro Education, 60*(2), 170–80.

Bishop, R. S. (1990). Mirrors, windows, and sliding glass doors. *Perspectives, 6*(3), ix–xi. Retrieved from https://scenicregional.org/wp-content/uploads/2017/08/Mirrors-Windows-and-Sliding-Glass-Doors.pdf

Conference on College Composition and Communication (CCCC). (1974). Students' right to their own language. *College Composition and Communication, 25*. Retrieved from http://www.ncte.org/library/NCTEFiles/Groups/CCCC/NewSRTOL.pdf

Davis, A. Y. (1981). *Women, race & class*. New York, NY: Random House.

Division of Rare and Manuscript Collections, Carl A. Kroch Library, Cornell University. (2002). In their own words: Slave narratives. In *"I will be heard!": Abolitionism in America*. Retrieved from http://rmc.library.cornell.edu/abolitionism/narratives.htm

Freire, P. (1970). *Pedagogy of the oppressed*. New York, NY: Continuum.

Freire, P. (1998). *Teachers as cultural workers: Letters to those who dare teach.* Boulder, CO: Westview Press.

Hermino Hernandez et al. v. Driscoll Consolidated Independent School District (DCISD) et al., CA 1384 (1957). Retrieved from https://catalog.archives.gov/id/26174936

Hill, M. L. (2016). *Nobody: Casualties of America's war on the vulnerable, from Ferguson to Flint and beyond.* New York, NY: Atria Books.

Hirsch, E. D. Jr. (1987). *Cultural literacy: What every American needs to know.* New York, NY: Houghton Mifflin.

hooks, b. (1994). *Teaching to transgress.* New York: Routledge.

McCarty, T. L. (2002). *A place to be Navajo: Rough Rock and the struggle for self-determination in Indigenous schooling.* New York, NY: Routledge.

McKissack, P. C. (2001). *Goin' someplace special* (J. Pinkney, Illus.). New York, NY: Atheneum Books for Young Readers.

National Council of Teachers of English. (2014). *NCTE beliefs about the students' right to write.* Retrieved from http://www2.ncte.org/statement/students-right-to-write/

National Council of Teachers of English. (2018). *The students' right to read.* Retrieved from http://www2.ncte.org/statement/righttoreadguideline/

Privilege. (n.d.). *Merriam-Webster.* Retrieved July 20, 2018, from https://www.merriam-webster.com/dictionary/privilege

Responsibility. (n.d.). *Merriam-Webster.* Retrieved July 20, 2018, from https://www.merriam-webster.com/dictionary/responsibility

Right. (n.d.). *Merriam-Webster.* Retrieved July 20, 2018, from https://www.merriam-webster.com/dictionary/right

Searcy, D. (2011, April 19). Voting: A right, a privilege, or a responsibility? *Right to Vote* [Blog]. FairVote. Retrieved from http://www.fairvote.org/voting-a-right-a-privilege-or-a-responsibility

Souto-Manning, M. (2010). *Freire, teaching, and learning: Culture circles across contexts.* New York, NY: Peter Lang.

Souto-Manning, M. (2019). Toward praxically-just transformations: Interrupting racism in teacher education. *Journal of Education for Teaching, 45*(1), 97–113.

Souto-Manning, M., & Yoon, H. S. (2018). *Rethinking early literacies: Reading and rewriting worlds.* Abingdon, UK: Routledge.

Walker, V. S. (2009). Foreword. In M. T. Fisher, *Black literate lives: Historical and contemporary perspectives* (pp. xv–xix). New York, NY: Routledge.

Children's Books

Ada, A. F. (1993). *Me llamo María Isabel* (K. Dyble Thompson, Illus.). New York, NY: Atheneum Books for Young Readers.

Ada, A. F. (2011). *Nacer bailando* (G. M. Zubizarreta, Illus.). New York, NY: Atheneum Books for Young Readers.

Ewald, W. (2002). *The best part of me: Children talk about their bodies in pictures and words.* Boston, MA: Little, Brown.

Myers, W. D. (2009). *Looking like me* (C. Myers, Illus.). New York, NY: Egmont.

Annotated Bibliography

Here is a list of resources we have found helpful in our journey to uphold students' rights to read, to write, and to speak their own language.

Some Favorite Teacher Books

Au, Wayne, editor
Rethinking Multicultural Education: Teaching for Racial and Cultural Justice, 2nd ed.
Milwaukee: Rethinking Schools, 2014

This book features the best articles dealing with race and culture in the classroom that have appeared in the *Rethinking Schools* magazine. Moving beyond a simplistic focus on heroes and holidays, foods and festivals, *Rethinking Multicultural Education* demonstrates a powerful vision of antiracist, social justice education. Practical, rich in story, and analytically sharp, this book reclaims multicultural education as part of a larger struggle for justice and against racism, colonization, and cultural oppression in schools and society.

Barbian, Elizabeth, Grace Cornell Gonzales, and Pilar Mejia, editors
Rethinking Bilingual Education: Welcoming Home Languages in Our Classrooms
Milwaukee: Rethinking Schools, 2017

How do we bring a social justice curriculum into our bilingual classrooms? How can we honor our students' native languages, even when we don't teach in a bilingual setting? How do we involve diverse groups of parents in our classrooms and schools? What can we learn from Indigenous language immersion about the integral relationship between language and culture? How do we elevate the status of nondominant languages when there is so much pressure to prioritize English? These are some of the important questions addressed by this book. *Rethinking Bilingual Education* comprises chapters portraying a variety of ways that teachers can bring students' home languages into their classrooms through powerful examples of social justice curricula taught by bilingual teachers. Additionally, it offers ideas and strategies for honoring students' languages in schools with no bilingual program.

Butler-Wall, Annika, Kim Cosier, Rachel L. S. Harper, Jeff Sapp, Jody Sokolower, and Melissa Bollow Tempel, editors
Rethinking Sexism, Gender, and Sexuality
Milwaukee: Rethinking Schools, 2016

Rethinking Sexism, Gender, and Sexuality is filled with inspiring, from-the-ground stories about practical ways to include LGBTQ+ content in the curriculum, make it a part of an approach to social justice, and create classrooms and schools that nurture all children and their families.

Delpit, Lisa
"Multiplication Is for White People": Raising Expectations for Other People's Children
New York: The New Press, 2012

Delpit reflects on two decades of reform efforts—including No Child Left Behind legislation, standardized testing, the creation of alternative teacher certification paths, and the charter school movement—that have still left a generation of poor children of color feeling that high academic achievement isn't for them. In chapters covering primary, middle, and high school, as well as college, Delpit concludes that it's not that difficult to explain the persistence of the achievement gap. She outlines a blueprint for raising expectations for "other people's children," based on the simple premise that multiplication—and every aspect of advanced education—is for everyone.

Dunbar-Ortiz, Roxanne (adapted by Jean Mendoza and Debbie Reese)
An Indigenous Peoples' History of the United States for Young People
Boston: Beacon Press, 2019

Addressing the miseducation of teachers as it pertains to the history they learned in schools, this book examines the legacy of Indigenous peoples' resistance, resilience, and unwavering battle against imperialism over the course of 400 years. Roxanne Dunbar-Ortiz reveals the roles that settler colonialism and policies of American Indian genocide played in forming America's national identity. In this version, the original academic text has been brilliantly adapted by Debbie Reese and Jean Mendoza for middle grade and young adult readers. It includes discussion topics, archival images, original maps, recommendations for further reading, and other materials, encouraging teachers to think critically about their own place in history. This book is key for anyone teaching in the pursuit of justice, offering important (albeit tenaciously invisiblized) historical accounts. (adapted from book description)

Emdin, Christopher
For White Folks Who Teach in the Hood . . . and the Rest of Y'All Too: Reality Pedagogy and Urban Education
Boston: Beacon Press, 2016

Christopher Emdin offers a new lens on an approach to teaching and learning in urban schools. He begins by taking to task the perception of urban youth of color as unteachable, and he challenges educators to embrace and respect each student's culture and to reimagine the classroom as a site where roles are reversed and students become the experts in their own learning. Putting forth his theory of "reality pedagogy," Emdin provides practical tools for unleashing the brilliance and eagerness of youth and educators alike. He demonstrates the importance of creating a family structure and building communities within the classroom using culturally relevant strategies such as hip-hop music and call-and-response,

and connecting the experiences of urban youth to Indigenous populations globally. Melding real stories with theory, research, and practice, Emdin demonstrates how reality pedagogy benefits urban youth of color by fostering truly transformative education.

Ladson-Billings, Gloria
The Dreamkeepers: Successful Teachers of African American Students, 2nd ed.
San Francisco: Jossey-Bass, 2009

In *The Dreamkeepers*, Ladson-Billings explores: Who are the successful teachers of African American students? What do they do? And how can we learn from them? Her portraits of eight exemplary teachers who differ in personal style and methods but share an approach to teaching that affirms and strengthens cultural identity are inspiring and full of hope. Written in three voices—that of an African American scholar and researcher, an African American teacher, and an African American parent and active community member—this book remixes scholarship and storytelling (summary adapted from the front flap of the first edition). In the second edition, Ladson-Billings revisits the eight teachers who were profiled in the first edition and introduces us to new teachers who are current exemplars of good teaching. *The Dreamkeepers* challenges us to envision intellectually rigorous and culturally relevant classrooms that have the power to improve the lives of not just African American students, but all children. This new edition also includes questions for reflection.

Ryan, Caitlin, and Jill M. Hermann-Wilmarth
Reading the Rainbow: LGBTQ-Inclusive Literacy Instruction in the Elementary Classroom
New York: Teachers College Press, 2018

Drawing on examples of teaching from elementary school classrooms, this book explains why LGBTQ+-inclusive literacy instruction is possible, relevant, and necessary in grades K–5. The authors show how expanding the English language arts curriculum to include representations of

LGBTQ+ people and themes will benefit all students, allowing them to participate in a truly inclusive classroom. The text describes three different approaches that address the limitations, pressures, and possibilities that teachers in various contexts face around these topics. The authors make clear what LGBTQ+-inclusive literacy teaching can look like in practice.

Souto-Manning, Mariana
Multicultural Teaching in the Early Childhood Classroom: Approaches, Strategies, and Tools, Preschool–2nd Grade
New York: Teachers College Press, 2013

This book features an array of approaches, strategies, and tools for teaching multiculturally in the early years. It features (a) multicultural education in action, including the everyday issues and tensions experienced by children and their families; (b) powerful vignettes from diverse settings, including Head Start, preschool, kindergarten, first- and second-grade classrooms throughout the United States; and (c) a list of multicultural children's books and resources for further reading.

Souto-Manning, Mariana, Carmen Lugo Llerena, Jessica Martell, Abigail Salas Maguire, and Alicia Arce-Boardman
No More Culturally Irrelevant Teaching
Portsmouth: Heinemann, 2018

Every child is a cultural being with a unique history and rich cultural practices—a member of communities in and outside of school. Yet too many children spend their days inside classrooms where they rarely find their voices, values, and cultural practices reflected in curriculum materials, much less embraced and sustained through teaching practices. In this book, four teachers who teach in richly diverse classrooms and have studied culturally relevant pedagogy for years with researcher Mariana Souto-Manning share specific practices, strategies, and tools that make their teaching culturally relevant.

Souto-Manning, Mariana, and Jessica Martell
Reading, Writing, and Talk: Inclusive Teaching Strategies for Diverse Learners, K–2
New York: Teachers College Press, 2016

This book introduces a variety of inclusive strategies for teaching language and literacy in kindergarten through second grade. Readers are invited into classrooms where racially, culturally, and linguistically diverse children's experiences, unique strengths, and expertise are supported and valued. Chapters focus on oral language, reading, and writing development and include diverse possibilities for culturally relevant and inclusive teaching. Featured teaching strategies foster academic success, cultural competence, and critical consciousness—leading students to read their worlds and question educational and societal inequities. The examples and strategies portrayed will help educators expand their thinking and repertoires regarding what is possible—and needed—in the language and literacy education curriculum. Unique in its focus on equitable, fully inclusive, and culturally relevant language and literacy teaching, this important book will help K–2 teachers (re)think and (re)conceptualize their own practices.

Souto-Manning, Mariana, and Haeny S. Yoon
Rethinking Early Literacies: Reading and Rewriting Worlds
New York: Routledge, 2018

Rethinking Early Literacies honors the identities of young children as they read, write, speak, and play across various spaces, in and out of pre/school. The book highlights the language resources and tools that children cultivate from families, communities, and peers in spite of narrow curricular mandates and policies in schools. The chapters feature children's linguistic flexibility with multiple languages, creative appropriation of popular culture, participation in community literacy practices, and social negotiation in the context of play. Throughout the book, the authors critically reframe what it means to be literate in contemporary society, specifically discussing the role of educators in theorizing and rethinking language ideologies for practice. Issues influencing early childhood education in trans/national contexts are forefronted (e.g., racism, immigration rights, readiness), with a call to support and sustain communities of color.

Children's Books

The We Need Diverse Books website (https:// diversebooks.org/resources/where-to-find-diverse-books/) includes an extensive list of websites that offer recommendations for diverse books under the following categories:

- African, African American
- American Indian
- Book Awards
- Disabilities
- Islam
- Jewish
- LGBTQ+
- Latinx
- Multicultural
- Social Justice

All of the sites we have used to find and evaluate children's books are included in this list. We hope you will enjoy this resource as much as we do.

Websites

Center for Racial Justice in Education
https://centerracialjustice.org/

Formerly known as Border Crossers, the Center for Racial Justice in Education trains and empowers educators to dismantle patterns of racism and injustice in schools and communities. "We envision a world where all young people learn and thrive in racially equitable, liberating, and empowering educational spaces." The center holds a number of workshops and trainings, which engage educators in explorations of race and racism with K–12 students.

Early Childhood Education Assembly of NCTE
https://www.earlychildhoodeducationassembly .com/

The Early Childhood Education Assembly of NCTE offers resources for educators focusing on antiracist learning and teaching. To support early childhood educators engaging deliberately in focused antiracist work, the group offers an array of resources that serve as impetus for teacher, staff, family, and community conversations, as well as professional development focused on awareness and action. These resources include but are not limited to "African American Histories: Curricular Resources and Information to Build Teachers' Background Knowledge," "Africa's Influence on the World's Knowledge," "Conversations about Race for Adults," "Understanding Bias, Privilege, and Profiling," and "Race Talk in the Early Childhood Classroom."

Gender & Family Project (GFP)
https://www.ackerman.org/

GFP, under the umbrella of the Ackerman Institute for the Family, provides gender-affirmative services, training, and research for educators and mental health and health providers, seeking to promote gender inclusivity as a form of social justice in all the systems involved in the life of families, including schools.

Living Undocumented
https://livingundocumented.com/

The Living Undocumented series consists of two documentaries produced and directed by City College of New York Professor Tatyana Kleyn: the 2012 film *Living Undocumented: High School, College and Beyond*, which captures the realities of undocumented youth in New York City and offers helpful information regarding documentation and immigration, and *Still Living Undocumented: Five Years Later*, a sequel that follows three individuals from the first film to see how DACA, Deferred Action for Childhood Arrivals, which is in jeopardy under a new federal administration, impacted their lives. Both documentaries are intended for all audiences, and we have used them with elementary students. The website states that the accompanying teaching and resource guides for students and educators are especially useful for secondary schools, but we have found them to be invaluable and have adapted them for the elementary grades.

Rethinking Schools

https://www.rethinkingschools.org/

Rethinking Schools began as a local effort to address problems identified in our book as obstacles to upholding students' rights to read and write, such as basal readers, standardized testing, and textbook-dominated curricula. Since then, Rethinking Schools has grown into a nationally prominent publisher of educational materials, including the *Rethinking Schools* magazine; *The New Teacher Book*; and *Planning to Change the World*, a planning book for justice-focused educators. Its website offers a wealth of materials, including books and lesson plans. Rethinking Schools remains firmly committed to equity and to the vision that public education is central to democracy. Rethinking Schools and its resources focus on problems facing urban schools, particularly pertaining to racism and entangled forms of bigotry.

Teaching Tolerance

https://www.tolerance.org/

Teaching Tolerance is a project of the Southern Poverty Law Center, its core goals to "foster inclusiveness, reduce bias, and promote educational equity" for K–12 students in the United States. Its mission is to help teachers and schools educate children and youth to be active participants in a diverse democracy. Teaching Tolerance provides free resources to educators—teachers, administrators, counselors and other practitioners—who work with children from kindergarten through high school. The materials offered can be used to supplement the curriculum, to inform teaching practices, and to create civil and inclusive school communities where children are respected, valued, and welcome participants. Teaching

Tolerance emphasizes social justice and espouses an antibias approach, offering classroom resources (including lesson plans), professional development, and publications focused on fostering social justice. Topics addressed include race and ethnicity, religion, ability, class, immigration, gender and sexual identity, bullying and bias, and rights and activism.

Zinn Education Project

https://www.zinnedproject.org/

The Zinn Education Project promotes and supports the use of Howard Zinn's bestselling book *A People's History of the United States* and other materials for teaching people's history in middle and high school classrooms across the country. The website features a rich database of resources, searchable by theme, time period, reading level, and format, and offers hundreds of free classroom lessons.

Professional Organizations

Early Childhood Education Assembly (ECEA)

https://www.earlychildhoodeducationassembly .com/

The Early Childhood Education Assembly is a vibrant group of teachers, teacher educators, researchers, and educational leaders concerned with issues related to the languages and literacies of children ages birth through eight, their families, and their communities. Under the leadership of Vivian Vasquez (2009–2011), Mariana Souto-Manning (2011–2013), and Dinah Volk (2013–2015), it has also become a space of advocacy that works as an official assembly within the National Council of Teachers of English. ECEA strives to encourage field-based research and theorized practice in the teaching of early childhood education across cultural and linguistic contexts; develop and promote equitable, culturally relevant and sustaining teaching in early childhood classrooms; develop and promote practices that lead to a more racially, ethnically, socially, and linguistically diverse teaching force in early childhood; and address issues of discrimination in the education of young children, including racism and entangled forms of bigotry pertaining to hierarchies of power in society associated with ethnicity, class, language, gender, sexual orientation, religion/faith, family structures, and dis/abilities. It offers powerful professional development opportunities for those interested in language, literacies, and equity in early childhood education.

National Council of Teachers of English (NCTE)
http://www2.ncte.org/

NCTE is a US-based professional organization dedicated to "improving the teaching and learning of English and the language arts at all levels of education [early childhood to college]." Since 1911, NCTE has provided an array of valuable opportunities for teachers to continue their professional growth throughout their careers. Its mission is as follows: "The Council promotes the . development of literacy, the use of language to construct personal and public worlds and to achieve full participation in society, through the learning and teaching of English and the related arts and sciences of language." NCTE holds a yearly convention each November.

New York Collective of Radical Educators (NYCoRE)
http://www.nycore.org/

NYCoRE is a group of public school educators and allies committed to fighting for social justice in our school system and society at large by organizing and mobilizing teachers, developing curriculum, and working with community, parent, and student organizations. NYCoRE comprises educators who believe that education is an integral part of social change and that teachers' commitment to and struggle for justice does not end when the school day does. NYCoRE sponsors a yearly conference in New York City, has a valuable listserv, and sponsors a variety of projects.

Index